Driving to Greenland

Peter Stark

BURFORD BOOKS

To my mother and father, who first propped me up in the snow,
and to my grandfather

COPYRIGHT © 1994 BY PETER STARK
ALL RIGHTS RESERVED. NO PART OF THIS BOOK MAY BE
REPRODUCED IN ANY MANNER WITHOUT THE EXPRESS
WRITTEN CONSENT OF THE PUBLISHER, EXCEPT IN THE
CASE OF BRIEF EXCERPTS IN CRITICAL REVIEWS AND
ARTICLES. ALL INQUIRIES SHOULD BE ADDRESSED TO:
BURFORD BOOKS, PO BOX 388,
SHORT HILLS, NJ 07078

PRINTED IN THE UNITED STATES OF AMERICA
DESIGN BY KATHY KIKKERT
10 9 8 7 6 5 4 3 2 1

LIBRARY OF CONGRESS CATALOGING-IN-PUBLICATION DATA
STARK, PETER, 1954-
DRIVING TO GREENLAND / PETER STARK.
P.   CM.
ORIGINALLY PUBLISHED: NEW YORK :
LYONS & BURFORD, C1994. WITH NEW INTROD.
ISBN 1-58080-066-1 (PBK.)
1. STARK, PETER, 1954-   . 2. SKIERS—
UNITED STATES—BIOGRAPHY.   3. WINTER SPORTS.
4. GREENLAND—DESCRIPTION AND TRAVEL.   I. TITLE.
[GV854.2.S83A3   1998]
796.93'092—DC21
[B]   98-27362   CIP

SOME OF THE PIECES IN THIS BOOK HAVE PREVIOUSLY
APPEARED IN MAGAZINES, AS FOLLOWS:

"LEAPS OF FAITH"—*OUTSIDE*, JANUARY 1985
"SLIDING TO GLORY"—*OUTSIDE*, DECEMBER 1985
"FEAR OF FALLING"—*OUTSIDE*, NOVEMBER 1987
"DEAN OF FLOW"—*OUTSIDE*, NOVEMBER 1993
"DRIVING TO GREENLAND" (ORIGINALLY TITLED
"GONE BOREAL")—*OUTSIDE*, FEBRUARY 1992
"LAND OF FIRE AND ICE"—*ISLANDS*, OCTOBER 1985
"A KINDE OF STRANGE FISHE"
—*SMITHSONIAN*, NOVEMBER 1992
"A SHORT WALK IN THE FIRNSPIEGEL"
—*OUTSIDE*, SCH. NOVEMBER 1994
"THE SEARCH FOR THE PERFECT SLED"
—*SMITHSONIAN*, DECEMBER 1987
"THE CARE AND USE OF PERFECT ICE"
—*OUTSIDE*, JANUARY 1991
"THE ICE LEAGUE"—*OUTSIDE*, JANUARY 1987

Contents

Acknowledgments

Literally hundreds of people have helped me in the course of researching and writing the pieces that appear in this collection. I feel a special debt to the generosity of the people of Northern Greenland, and particularly to Hans Jensen and Vittus Qujaukitsoq; in Iceland, Sigurdur Einarsson was of invaluable help. Mark Bryant of *Outside* Magazine got behind many of these pieces from their inception, as did Marlane Liddell and Constance Bond at *Smithsonian* and Connie Bourassa-Shaw at *Islands*. Peter Burford of Lyons & Burford saw the possibilities of a collection that centered on snow and ice and helped give it shape. My fellow writers in Missoula and at Point Wilson have provided endless support and direction over the years. Finally, this book would not exist without the encouragement and companionship, not to mention intrepidness, of my wife, Amy Ragsdale.

Introduction
to the 1998 Edition

When I first came up with the idea to assemble this collection I quickly realized how little has been published about the season of winter compared to summer. How few books there are about winter sports compared to those about football, baseball, or track; how few about the snowy Arctic compared to the weighty shelves of volumes published about balmier climes like, say, southern France; how few about the miraculous substances we call snow and ice compared to the lavish selection about summer pastimes such as gardening.

It's my theory that this is partly because most books are published by people who live in large cities—and people who live in large cities tend to hate snow and ice. It clogs the street, it blocks the sidewalks, it causes you to slip on your slick leather soles and smack a hip bone against ice-coated concrete. But there are millions of people—many who indeed live in cities and others in more rural areas—who love winter and whose passion for it has gone largely unrecognized.

That these lovers of winter exist—and that a few haters of winter might be converted—was the original inspiration for this collection. The reception given to the hardcover edition when it appeared four years ago proved that my theory wasn't entirely wrong. I'm pleased that Burford Books is now making Driving to Greenland available in paperback, and hope that it might help more readers see the light about the coldest, darkest season.

—Peter Stark

A Life Built on Snow

From my earliest memories I associated my grandfather with ice, and my father I associated with snow. My grandfather was a skater and an iceboater while my father, as well as my mother, was a fine skier. Soon after we four children were old enough to walk, he and my mother clamped miniature skis to our stubby little legs, propped us like rag dolls between their legs, and glided us gently down the baby slope at the local ski hill. My father loved a good snowfall and talked about them with a passion he reserved for few subjects. "Just *look* at the way it's coming down," he'd burst out to me as the fat flakes danced through our yard lights on a wintry evening. "Tomorrow's going to be a *great day* at the hill!"

It's a good thing I became acquainted so early with snow and ice, because at the time I wasn't doing all that well on dry land. Where I grew up, near a small lake in southern Wisconsin, most of the other boys were a year or two older than myself and I was the straggler. Shy and fearful, yet wanting to belong in that desperate way that small boys do, I was at times the butt of their pranks such as the game they called "ditch" where the object was for everyone suddenly to run off and hide from the ditchee, a role I found myself in often and unhappily. Very young, however, I discovered that the slick surfaces of snow and ice are the great equalizers and that a four-year-old boy riding a sled undergoes the exact same rate of gravitational acceleration (32 feet per second/per second) as a six-year-old boy. On snow and ice, I found I could easily keep up with the older boys and, with a little finesse, blow right past them.

I like to think I became a snow and ice specialist by the age of four or five. Winter became my private world just as some children find theirs in a special corner of the garden or attic. I collected the secrets of snow and ice the way that other boys collected snakes and rocks, and savored the power of ice heaves and avalanches like other boys keened after fighter planes and large guns. This was a problem, because there *are* no avalanches in the cornfields of Wisconsin. I thus built my own by stacking large cardboard blocks into a cornice-like ledge at the top of the basement stairs and, having thoughtfully distributed toy Green Bay Packer football helmets to them for head protection against the concrete wall at the bottom, lured my younger brother and sister to join me on this shaky perch until it collapsed under our weight and swept us down in an avalanche of cardboard.

Each winter I gained a little more confidence, and the best snow and ice lessons I learned carried over from winter to the other seasons. There was the one, for example, I acquired during our first family ski vacation to Aspen in the early 1960s when I was about ten, and Aspen was still a rickety old mining town. A kindly instructor named Gretl taught me to employ the sudden, disconcerting upthrust of a mogul to *turn* my skis rather than throw me down—to *use* rough terrain to my advantage rather than fight it—a lesson that many skiers (and many people) don't learn in a lifetime. Back at home on the lake, my grandfather, founder of the family's small candy-manufacturing firm of which my father was president, educated me about ice: "You know enough not to listen to what most people say about ice, don't you?" he'd ask, in a manner both bulldoggish and warm. "You know enough not to be afraid of it," he'd say, as if to reassure himself that I wasn't what he called a "sissy."

He'd love to race iceboats on Lake Mendota as a student at the University of Wisconsin in the teens and had fallen through the ice as often and as casually as other people might trip over the hall runner. His instructions for extracting myself from any jagged hole in which I happened to find myself included keeping calm (that was the most important thing, not to panic), swimming back the way I had come until I reached solid ice, and then wallowing up onto it like a walrus. These all were useful lessons, but his most valuable teaching didn't give a whit for safety. I didn't really grasp its import until years later, when one evening at a family dinner as I sat at his end of the big mahogany table he asked me, totally out of the blue, if I believed in God.

As I stumbled around for an answer, he confided that he himself had to believe in *some* kind of god because of what he knew about ice. Water, he explained, is almost unique among substances in that it *expands* when it freezes. If this single detail of the grand plan were askew and those tiny hexagonal ice crystals *contracted* like other substances as they froze, there would be one gawdawful mess, as he put it, because ice would sink to the bottom of the seas instead of floating, eventually flood the continents, and the human species would not have advanced any further than a swimming protozoan.

This was my grandfather's ice-crystal-as-proof-of-God theorum, and what it finally taught me was not to embrace God but to see ice and snow as metaphors for something larger than themselves, a task to which their very blankness and otherworldliness suit them perfectly. Of course, I didn't quite see them this way back then. I wasn't into metaphors yet. I was a dorky fourth or fifth grader in glasses whose irreverent little sister called him "Ernie," after the gawkish youngest brother on "My Three Sons," and when the other boys in school called me "four eyes." They played tag football after school and I didn't. My mother asked if I wanted to participate but I shook my head no, for no reason that I can think of except that I was frightened. "You're our skier," she said, and as they played football and I walked home from school on those autumn afternoons, feeling awkward and outcast, I consoled myself with the thought that, come winter, I could out-sled, out-ski, out-skate, out-anything them all. This boy's pure joy in winter, I now understand, was all bound up with this pure need for power.

Everything in my life changed when I took up ski racing, an event that fortunately coincided with puberty and helped channel my vital energies into slalom courses instead of girlie magazines, which is where some of my classmates were busily expending theirs. I'd entered my first race because another boy I admired raced. I did well and liked it, and received high praise from my father. A former football star, he'd no doubt long ago abandoned any hope of making a halfback out of me, and this interest in competitive sports on my part must have been a welcome surprise to him.

I took up racing with a vengeance and among other racers felt, for a while at least, that I really belonged. Shortly after, I also discovered the world of literature—and would frown in deep concentration over the "hidden meanings" of poems—but I kept these powerful literary weapons close to my chest, out of sight of my classmates. Thus armed, I survived the treacherous jungles of high school. I'd been brusquely relegated to the "out" crowd when I'd entered a new school in the seventh grade; by the eighth grade, through hard work I'd accumulated enough bad-boy behavior to be admitted to the distant margins of the "in" crowd. Then, in the ninth grade, seemingly in a blinding flash, my passions erupted and my life changed: this was the year I became serious about ski racing and literature, and at the same time took up with a girlfriend a grade older than I was. She was so unequivocally cool in her suede miniskirts and long blonde hair that simply through her presence at my side I knew I had transcended the crowds altogether, in or out or in-between.

How I came to have a girlfriend like this so suddenly is hard to say, but in large part I attribute it to a sort of self-possession—not to mention a certain self-absorption—that overcame me when I took up ski racing and literature. Much of our relationship unfolded in long, intimate, hushed phone conversations that I conducted from frigid, northern motel rooms. Almost every Friday afternoon throughout the winter we racers would pile into somebody's parents' station wagon crammed full of duffels and ski boots, and drive eight or ten hours north to the races held in Michigan's Upper Peninsula.

Although I was good at ski racing and have a heap of medals to prove it, I would have much preferred my girlfriend's warm embrace to shivering on some bitterly windswept, North Woods hilltop waiting my turn to enter the starting gate. What I truly loved were not the races but the practice sessions on our home hill. For one thing, they kept me closer to my girlfriend; for another, I saw a kind of art to running gates even then, when I wouldn't have dared mention art to my fellow racers for fear of being laughed off the course.

The image always comes up Japanese: my skis slashed turns between the bamboo poles of a slalom course like the quick, bold brushstrokes of Japanese ink painting. The painter concentrates on manipulating the angle at which the brush attacks the paper, the ski racer on manipulating the angle at which the sharp steel ski edge cuts through the snow. Looking back, I find it staggering to think how many thousands of hours of my life I've spent manipulating an *edge* like this through a *medium* of some sort—ski through snow, skate across ice, even canoe through water. This action, this gliding along a continuum, differs profoundly from most other sports as well as from our daily lives, in which we move dot to dot, cudgeling the ground with club-like feet.

Taking a cue from my grandfather's vision of ice, I find all sorts of metaphors along this continuum, but the one I like best touches on grace and chaos in the guise of a figure skater who glides through, let's say, a one-footed turn. Viewed from a distance, that skate blade presents a picture of smoothly arcing grace, but on a molecular level all hell breaks loose as those tiny ice crystals bend and shatter and melt under the steel edge, both lubricating its forward glide and wedging against it so that it doesn't slip laterally. I relish this destructive, molecular rip of the skate blade through ice just as the small boy relished the rumbling might of the avalanche. But I now prefer that this kind of icy chaos serves a figure skater's grace instead of smashing forests and sweeping away villages. I account for this change in attitude by subsequent events in my own life; there came a time when I hoped that out of chaos, grace would somehow emerge.

In my sophomore year at Dartmouth College snow and ice—the gods to which I'd paid homage—finally turned against me. At least that's the way it appeared to me at the time. My faults, the ones that I can see, probably were sins of hubris: my belief that I was a better skier, knew more about literature and about life, than my geeky classmates. This belief wasn't entirely without foundation, or so I like to think—at least the part about life. I'd managed to graduate a year early from high school in Wisconsin by carrying a load of accelerated courses and was accepted a year early at Dartmouth, long famous for its ski team and winter sports program. As my high-school classmates busied themselves with yearbook projects and statistics courses, I spent what would have been my senior year bumming around Europe's ski resorts armed with a backpack and a stiff pair of Kneissel racing skis.

You have to understand that this was 1971, when a whole youth culture wandered all over Europe with backpacks, albeit few as young as I was. I picked up odd jobs here and there, working first as a *pistendienst*—trail crew worker—at a ski resort in the Austrian Alps, and then I hustled gigs as an underground ski instructor in the Matterhorn's shadow at the famous Swiss mountain village of Zermatt. "Underground" meant out of sight of the hawkish eyes of the legitimate (and pricey) Swiss ski instructors who, it was rumored among my fellow long-haired ski bums, would break both your legs in addition to your skis if they caught you working their turf.

It was party time in the Alps, we were ski bums in paradise, and very quickly I came to fancy myself a very worldly young man. I met gracious, beautiful couples wintering in the Alps from lowland countries like Denmark and England; they took me under their wings, the men buying me drinks in the candlelit clubs and their perfumed, cashmere-clad women holding me close when we danced. I was the pet American ski bum, another bit of local color like the frescoes in the village chapel, and I played up the role. A young American male wandering around Europe in those Vietnam years was naturally suspected to be on the lam from the draft, and the women tossed me their liberal sympathies as if they were lace handkerchiefs. Worldly young man that I wanted to be, I kept up a mysterious silence on this topic, too embarrassed to reveal that, just going on eighteen, I still wasn't *old* enough to be drafted.

I lived in the attic of a pension, read Dostoyevski—partly out of pretentiousness, partly to keep my hand in the literary game, and each day I religiously ran slalom gates to train for the ski team at Dartmouth, which I hoped to join the following year. What I really could have used was a lot less nightlife, and some serious ski competition. My finest moment on skis that I recall from those delirious days didn't occur on a race course at all but in Zermatt when I met a woman—a girl, really, a year or two older than I was—who skied well enough to race on the U.S. Ski Team but had quit competition and now was bumming around Europe as I was. We did up the nightclubs of Zermatt but it's that first morning together that I remember so vividly—making love as the slow yellow sun shone through the windows of her dark, ramshackle old chalet and threw a band of warm light across the starched Swiss sheets.

It had stormed for the past several days, but that morning it cleared off. Three feet of fresh powder snow lay sparkling in the sun. We quickly dressed, ran through the streets filled with jingling horsedrawn sleighs, and grabbed the Gornergrat train up the mountain. She'd spent a lifetime on hardpacked race courses and didn't know how to ski deep powder, but I did. She stood below and watched as I skied a huge, virgin headwall of it. In that single run I suddenly felt the fullness of my power and loved the taste of it; with each turn I dolphined joyfully up, up, way UP out of the snow and arced airborne through the sunlight in a shower of crystal sparks before plunging down into the snow again.

She hugged me tightly through her parka when I reached her at the headwall's foot and said it was so beautiful to watch. I could hardly talk; I was out of my head with the sun and the powder and her and the night before and the Matterhorn's peak, which rose into the blue sky above it all. We skied together hard all that day, and the next and the next, stopping only to duck into mountaintop restaurants where sleek suntanners in chaises languorously sipped from thimble-like glasses. You could compare it to making love, swooping down a trail fast and hard in rhythm with a woman who skis so well, except things move much faster, and you're pumped with adrenaline and with the cold wind in your face; you play off each other's maneuvers—responding, teasing, suggesting—and off the rolls and dips of the mountain itself, which finally becomes a third partner in this act of union through high-speed motion.

I began my freshman year at Dartmouth the following fall after that heady year, and I don't know what sort of sophisticates and intellectuals I expected to encounter, but to my crashing disappointment my classmates struck me as pimply adolescents in high-school letter jackets. I wanted arts and letters and witty conversation, but Freshmen Week felt like some kind of summer camp. "This is kid stuff," I said in my arrogance, but I reluctantly played along with the game at first, fulfilling the freshmen requirements and slowly climbing my way into the middle ranks of the ski team. This proved to be no small task, as the best skiers at Dartmouth, stuck way up there in northern New England (the butt of snowshoe jokes by more urbane Ivy Leaguers), are of Olympic caliber.

During my sophomore year, the whole structure of my life came tumbling down. It was partly due to my realization that I was nowhere near an Olympic-caliber skier and would never be. This was the first hint at my limits—in effect, of my mortality. I wasn't alone in suddenly feeling the boundaries of life tighten and the first dim fear of mediocrity. When the great, idealistic bubble of the anti-war movement burst with the reelection of Richard Nixon in 1972, many college students suddenly stopped caring about the world and started caring about their careers. I pretended I didn't really give a shit about either, and so I drank beer in fraternity-house basements, having what I thought was fun.

The nation sank into a kind of collective depression as, each day, it learned more about its own limits: the OPEC states had formed their first oil cartel; the dark doings of Watergate had begun to unfold; and Vietnam was a disaster. As if internalizing the general malaise, my father became depressed quite literally, worrying even more deeply about losses in the family candy-manufacturing business, and then becoming convinced both he and it were going broke. Though not a large company, it carried a weighty family legacy that extended back to my great-grandfather, a German immigrant who, in the 1880s, had joined a candy firm in Milwaukee as a bookkeeper and eventually came to own half of it. The current company had been founded by my grandfather—the ice grandfather—and then turned over to my father.

With the turmoil in world events, sugar prices had gone through the roof, profits had vanished, and the steady old family company had begun to take deep losses as it never had before, with no relief in sight. One morning late in the fall of my sophomore year, I received a phone call from my mother. In the predawn hours my father had swallowed a bottle of sleeping pills, she said, then had a change of heart, jumped into the frigid, half-frozen lake to try to wake himself, and was rushed to the hospital in an ambulance, where he now lay in a coma, though the doctors expected him to recover. I wish I could remember exactly what I felt, but after that first, stomach-in-the-throat moment, mostly I

remember trying *not* to feel anything. In the interest of family pro-
priety, my mother asked that I not tell anyone about the incident.
My roommates were fixing breakfast in the kitchen of our apartment, and I tried to handle the phone call as calmly and matter of
factly as I could, and, true to my promise, I said nothing.

For a long time I didn't tell anyone about it and pushed down
inside of me whatever it was that I felt, not understanding, as I do
now, that what you try to bury in one vault of your heart inevitably surfaces elsewhere in another form. In the course of the
next few months, my confidence, now sagging and creaking like
an old chair under too much weight, collapsed into uncertainty,
my deftness gave way to frustration. At first I tried not to notice.
Then I did notice but pretended I was too jaded to care. Finally I
did care but it was too late to get back whatever it was that I'd lost.
I suddenly discovered that I couldn't do anything *right* anymore;
I got Ds in English literature, botched my relations with the
opposite sex, and—this is what made me wild with frustration—
was unable to manipulate that edge through that medium.

One moment stands out with crystalline clarity—a brilliant-
blue, below-zero January day on a ski slope at Stowe, Vermont.
The Dartmouth ski team had entered a giant slalom race, my best
event, on a particularly fast, icy course. To ski on icy snow demands total confidence because you absolutely must not lean
your body *toward* the safety of the hill but, against all instinct,
must lean *away* from the slope—which, on steep pitches, is like
hanging out a twentieth-story window and removing yours hands
from the sill. Only then can you drive enough weight onto your
downhill ski to make its steel edge bite into the slope and prevent
you from slipping off the icy mountain. The paradox is that, like

so many difficult tasks, if you don't commit yourself to it totally you will surely fail, but to commit yourself totally you must, psychologically, *know* that you will succeed.

In short, boldness works and timidity doesn't. This kind of confidence takes years to learn but you can unlearn it in an instant. I'd had trouble holding an edge in competition earlier that winter; I *knew* I could do better but I kept screwing up. This was the day—a fast giant slalom, my best event—when I was going to prove myself, get it all back, correct this suddenly wobbly course my life had taken. This was the day when I'd show them all—the coaches, the other racers, myself—that I had what it takes.

I don't remember skiing the beginning of that course; I recall only my anxiousness to ski it perfectly and a nagging worry whether I'd sharpened my edges enough the previous night to handle a particularly icy turn halfway down the mountain. I see the red and blue flags of the gates flashing past as I sweep into that worrisome turn, then feel the sudden, nauseating slip of my edge on the ice, my arms flailing in an attempt at recovery, the sharp slam as my hip hits the ice, and the long, hopeless, spinning fall down the mountainside as I futilely claw at the snow.

I wasn't hurt. I don't remember if I sprawled there in the snow and sobbed, sick with frustration and self-disgust, or if I only felt like it. Disgust for my idiotic, timid mistake of leaning into the hill for safety, disgust for not adequately preparing my edges, disgust for the whole stupid mess I'd made of my life. As I finally regained enough composure to crawl back up the slope, another competitor sailed easily through the tricky turn. He wore a number I recognized. I'd raced against him, and usually had beaten him quite easily, in high school in Wisconsin. He now also attended school in the East and raced for his college team. I watched from hands and knees as he receded rapidly downhill.

That was my last collegiate ski race. It was nearly ten years before I truly embraced the snow again, a decade on rough, dry, rocky ground. Not that I didn't try sooner. I still *wanted* to race that winter, but soon after Stowe, New England's winter rains poured down in torrents and canceled race after race along with any further hopes for redemption. I kicked at the melting slush and cursed the winter. I felt betrayed by winter, that it had let me down in this moment of need. Maybe, down in that inner vault of mine, I was actually feeling angry at and betrayed by my father for his suicide attempt, or by my mother for trying to hide it, or by myself for being so irresponsible in my life.

Looking back over these twenty years, I understand things that I didn't at the time. I was both the oldest son and oldest grandson and I knew those relationships entailed special responsibilities. My father and I weren't especially close but we weren't far apart either. He'd led an adventurous, wide-ranging youth on sailing ships and freighters. I admired his strength and boldness, although I probably wouldn't have admitted it then. I knew he was proud of me, and proud especially of my ski racing, because it was the language of competition that we had in common. I now understand that he and his pride in me formed a central pillar on which I balanced my young life. When he collapsed that day, the pillar toppled and shattered like a chunk of ice that breaks from a calving glacier, and I was left clawing at thin air. I hadn't bothered to build other pillars of my own, so I went crashing down, too. When the father became self-destructive, so did the son, and when the son didn't understand what was happening to him he blamed it on the bad weather. I still carry in my mind's eye a certain snowbank in a darkened lane in Hanover. It sits passively under a streetlight as a drizzly rain slowly erodes it into slushy puddles in the gutter—a cold, dripping metaphor for what might have been.

I mark the next years by winters in which I didn't participate. I quit school and spent that first snowless winter living on the cheap in India, eating opium, getting sick, and trying to figure out what I owed to whom to set my life straight. The question I wrestled with, first in the tropics of Goa and then in the shadow of the Himalayan mountains, was this: Should I join the family candy business where I could help out my father and my family, or pursue my own passions, which had to do with books? Were my obligations to my family or to myself? I felt I'd let everybody down and now I wanted to make damned sure I didn't screw up again. I wanted to know for certain which was the right choice, but I didn't know myself and no one else could tell me because I'd locked too much in that inner vault.

The second and third of my snowless winters I completed college. The fourth I spent in Boston, rising hours before dawn each morning in a shabby, unfurnished flat in hopes of discovering whether I possessed the discipline to write. At 9 A.M. I put away my typewriter and went off to my job as a "mechanic" in a ski shop, unable to let go of the skiing way of life even after I'd quit racing. That winter my father attempted suicide again—this time by lying down on a railroad track and curling up at the last instant as a freight train roared overhead, the engineer madly trying to bring it to a halt. (He had a flair for the dramatic even when he was depressed.) My older sister called me with the news. "I don't know if I can go through this again," I remember telling her. "I almost wish he'd succeeded."

When I later talked to him on the phone, however, he sounded absolutely, fatalistically down and empty and hollow. After I hung up I broke down and cried. This time they'd placed him in a hospital under psychiatric observation. He was then diagnosed as a manic-depressive and began treatment with what they called a miracle drug, lithium. That his action was the result of depression caused by a "chemical imbalance," as it was explained to me at the time, made me see his problems as a disease, or almost a mechanical malfunction, like a broken part in the washing machine. But most of all it made me see my father as simply human and as vulnerable as I.

The fifth and sixth of my snowless winters I came home to Wisconsin—not to join the family business, despite the way it gnawed at my sense of responsibility, but to attend graduate school in journalism at the University of Wisconsin. That second suicide attempt jolted me into changing the nature of my questions. Instead of asking to whom I was responsible, I began to ask how I'd be happy. I'd begun to see that you couldn't truly *be* responsible unless first you were happy.

My resolve slowly hardened but the snowless years didn't end that simply. After completing graduate school, I took a part-time reporter's job at a newspaper in Montana. I told people back home that I was interested in what I called "remote places," but what I should have said is that I needed to get the hell out of there, to get some distance from my family. Montana attracted me for other reasons, too: I had fond memories of the blue skies and deep snow from childhood spring vacations in the Colorado Rockies, and I hoped to find similar conditions in Montana. What I remember of those first months in Montana, however, is not winter but summer; not snow but the hot, dry, glaring western sun baking the living sanity out of both the stony mountains and my own head.

Six months into the job I lost my confidence as quickly as I'd let that edge slip at Stowe, but now my uncertainty focused on my writing. I became convinced—entirely without reason—that I might have libeled someone in a story I had written for an out-of-state newspaper. "This is ridiculous," I told myself, but I couldn't shake a terrible anxiety about my work. In retrospect, it appears obvious that this grew out of my guilt for making the break from my family and abandoning the family business. But I couldn't see that then. I became so uptight about writing that I couldn't set down a word without changing it six times. I continually second-guessed my reporting, wondering if I had got my facts right. I so desperately wanted to do things *right*. At night, I'd dream that I cradled a shotgun in my hands and didn't quite know how to use it, worrying that it might suddenly discharge and I'd inadvertently shoot someone, as if I were frightened of the hair-trigger power of journalism itself.

At its worst, when I began to imagine that someone might be listening into my phone calls or going through my notes, monitoring me—yet knowing at the same time that this was absurd—I simply took off, on the excuse that I was going trout fishing deep in the forests of central Idaho. Here, in the biggest stretch of wilderness in the lower forty-eight states, I figured I could, if necessary, disappear into the woods and reemerge months later as another person, sort of hatching out of the woods like a turtle from an egg. I eventually calmed down enough to abandon the tortoise plan. I went back to work. There my frustrations and anxieties overwhelmed me again. I wanted to quit, to walk away from journalism. I thought about going back to Wisconsin and working for the family business, forgetting this foolish notion of trying to write. But I realized that if I quit now I'd spend the rest of my life running, that if I didn't face up to it now I never would.

And so I stayed. I struggled through a hot, hot August when in Montana you can smell the distant forest fires and the sun hangs in a smoke-singed sky like a hot eye, watching you. The rock of the mountains itself appears to shrivel up like desiccated rawhide. I held on, fighting my anxiety, struggling with every word I wrote as August gave way to September and September eased into October. Then it finally happened: I woke one mid-October morning and the air was cold and clear. I looked out the window and saw that in the night the year's first snow had draped itself in a white veil halfway down the grassy hills. It was in that instant that I felt the first real loosening of the tight coils inside me; here was the world that I knew best and loved, creeping down the mountainsides to meet me.

There were great, deep snowstorms that winter, foot after foot of deep powder. I sought it out eagerly, but not so much for its celebrated floating sensation as for the chance to *fall*. Deep snow allowed me to let go—to abandon all control, to relax. Some chance mistake—a crossing of my ski tips, say—would send me tumbling head over heels down the slope in a cloud of white. I happily let myself go, gave myself over to it, cartwheeling as free and uncaring as a tumbleweed in a desert wind, or like a dog, or a child, or a grizzly bear who romps in the snow. The deep snows during the first Montana winter allowed me to ignore that debilitating, adult, self-consciousness that was whispering in my ear:

that I must do things *right*, that I mustn't make *mistakes*, that I must not *screw up* my life. If only for a few minutes or a few hours, all that snow let me say to that voice, "Fuck *YOU!*"

Surprisingly, it was in Montana that year that I first met people who really didn't know about or care for snow. Some had emigrated from states like California, others were Montana natives who'd grown up on ranches, where winter is regarded as one huge inconvenience, one that makes it harder for animals to graze. These people preferred the dusty, beery sports of softball and rodeo, and, for winter sport, if they were native Montanans, they'd happily drive 300 miles to watch a game of high school basketball. But winter was mainly the season in which they waited for spring, hunched over sports pages and stock reports like burrowed-in squirrels over a cache of nuts.

I tried to tell my friends that by ignoring winter they were missing out on one-quarter of life. When they did take up winter sports like skiing, I rarely saw in them the joy of winter that came so easily to me. They had to *work* at winter. I wondered whether to truly enjoy it you had to grow up in the heart of it. For me, the sports of summer and fall were difficult; I could never quite appreciate the self-contained beauty of baseball or master the infinite patience with which a native Montanan can sit still as a stone for hours in a cold woods, waiting for a deer to happen in front of his rifle barrel.

To love winter, to love anything or anybody, you must let go and give yourself over to it. But I still hadn't really reconciled myself with winter after that earlier quarrel; winter was still something I did on my days off from the serious work of life. This changed when, after two and a half years, I finally quit newspaper reporting and took up freelance writing. At first I pursued subjects that had a Montana angle but I was quickly drawn to ideas that would bring me in contact with snow and ice.

I was just starting out and still trying to land my first assignment with a major magazine when I got a sudden inspiration: to learn to ski jump under the guidance of the old jumpers of Norwegian descent on Michigan's Upper Peninsula, where I'd once raced. I happened to be returning to Wisconsin to visit my family over Christmas, a convenient opportunity to undertake this ski jumping business. An editor at *Outside* magazine expressed a strong interest in the ski-jumping story—stronger even than I'd hoped; he undoubtedly saw some of the dramatic possiblities (possibilities that I was trying my best to suppress) in a greenhorn like myself riding down the ski jump. Our negotiations dragged on for weeks, however, because he couldn't convince the other editors to make a firm commitment to the piece. By this time, I was back in the Midwest for Christmas and it was now or never for the ski jump. Finally I said, "The hell with them, I'll do it anyway, and write it and *then* try to sell it to them."

That was my first leap of faith. The second came a few days before I headed north from my parents' home in southern Wisconsin toward the Upper Peninsula. I attended a dinner party in Madison at the home of a former journalism professor of mine and became reacquainted with his daughter, whom I'd met briefly once before. She was visiting her family over Christmas from New York, where she was a modern dancer. She was beautiful, charming, and smart, and she even seemed to *like* me. When she mentioned that she loved to travel, I half-jokingly invited her to accompany me to Upper Michigan. To my great surprise— and partly my horror—she accepted.

By the time we finally got underway, I was nervous enough about my weekend in the North Country with the professor's daughter and about how to write this non-assignment for this major magazine, that the third leap of faith, the one where I was actually supposed to fly off the ski jump, began to look relatively simple by comparison. It wasn't, but that's another story. That first night was New Year's Eve, 1983, and we ate steaks at a supper club near Ironwood, an old bastion of ski jumping on the Wisconsin-Michigan border. The club had a nautical motif—don't ask me why, sitting out in the timber as it was—and a bar done up like a ship's prow with an aquarium set in the wall, where tropical fish swam lazily in a blue light. As midnight approached, the merrymakers in the bar donned their party hats and blew their horns, and we leaned closer over the table to talk to each other more intimately. The snow outside was piled four feet deep and was still falling, luscious and fluffy, and I, wrapping my arms around the world with a quieter version of the ebullience of the revelers in the bar, saw nothing but possibility everywhere I looked. In that single moment if at no other time in my life, I *knew* that I was happy.

Not guessing how close to the bone they were, the editors at *Outside* titled the piece "Leaps of Faith." They liked it enough that they commissioned me to write more winter-sports articles in the George Plimpton, amateur-out-of-his-depth vein, articles about learning to ride a luge sled or forerunning a World Cup downhill ski course. This is what launched me, literally at times, into writing about winter and snow and ice. As for the professor's daughter: ten years later Amy and I, now married, still mark that ski-jumping trip to the Upper Peninsula—our first date.

One thing I liked immediately about this kind of writing and reporting, about the frictionless surfaces of snow and ice, is that it demands absolute concentration, less as a matter of journalistic principle than of self-preservation. You note *exactly* how some-one fastens the bindings of his jumping skis, say, because you want to fasten yours in *exactly* the same manner lest they fall off your feet when you're in mid-air. I was plenty frightened many times but it's a different kind of scared than the scattered mind-lessness that I'd experienced at other times in my life, a very fo-cused scared. Once you're roaring down a tube of ice or a snowy mountainside at 60 or 70 miles per hour, sheathed in nothing but a thin skin of rubbery fabric, you don't have the luxury to think about anything except what's immediately in front of your hurtling body. No static—no doubts, no needs, nothing but total absorption in motion. It's as if your nervous system shifts over from the flickering circuitry of daily consciousness to older and deeper neural pathways, and you react as fast and instinctively as a deer that darts and dodges through thick woods.

But, after a while, this still wasn't enough. These so-called "thrill sports" represented only a narrow band of the world of snow and ice, and I wanted to throw my embrace wider around it, despite the way that this high-speed concentration exerted an almost meditative, calming effect on me.

Another calming influence exerted itself about then, when my father finally sold the family business, thankfully closing that door to me forever. Meanwhile, my younger brother started his own candy-manufacturing firm, helping to ensure that the family legacy didn't die. My father and the business had both prospered since he'd begun lithium treatment, and those depressions were long behind him. I could understand why he wanted to sell it; I saw the burden as well as the benefit that a family business could be, especially one that carried with it a legacy of several generations and the dependency of many mouths to feed. After my own losses of confidence, I could also understand some of the torment he must have gone through in his depressions. In an odd, backhand way, I was finally even grateful for those suicide attempts and difficult years I'd then experienced. They had strengthened me—liberated me to seek my own path rather than fall back on the predictable road that was already laid out for me.

When the business was sold, I began to look out to the world more. In particular, I began to look at all that snow and ice that lay to the far north. What really got me hooked was a flight from Reykjavík to Chicago, as I returned from researching a story on Iceland. We'd been airborne an hour or two, and I was munching peanuts and sipping beer when I casually pushed my forehead against the airplane window and looked down at a sight so stunning and hallucinatory that it became my Holy Grail. This was the east coast of Greenland, glowing like a brilliant, white planet in a blue-back ocean as deep as outer space. We flew inland and I pressed my face against the window to see ice that inundated the mountain valleys ever more deeply until only the highest stony peaks projected, like church steeples poking out of a snowy plain, and then they, too, were swallowed up in the huge blank dome of the Inland Ice. I remember thinking: this is the moment you're supposed to pledge that someday you'll return. A few years later on a warm June afternoon I began that return: Amy, her father, and I climbed into his aging VW van in Montana and headed due north on U.S. 93 with Greenland as our ultimate destination.

What surprised me about traveling north like that is not how big our planet is but how *small*. Usually I'd traveled on an east-west axis—to Europe, or to Asia—where neither the climate nor light change much with each thousand miles. But traveling north I could *feel*, on an almost hourly basis, the globe curving over toward the pole as the earth's surface metamorphosed from evergreen forest, to tundra, to that cap of white ice. Looking back toward the south, I suddenly grasped that we humans occupy a narrow, freakish warm belt that girds our planet's middle. And when I finally entered that deep, silent cold, I came to realize in a way I hadn't before that death lies just a single layer of clothing away, that our species is as perishable as a culture of bacteria that's gently warmed in a laboratory petri dish.

Even more remarkably, when we finally did land on Greenland's coast a mere 800 miles from the North Pole, we found people *living* there. These are the Polar, or Thule, Eskimos, the inhabitants of the northernmost villages in the world. Unlike the Canadian Eskimos to the southwest, the Polar Eskimos have banished the snowmobile from their hunting grounds and still rely on their traditional dogsleds and kayaks, and bring in narwhals with a hand-thrown, three-piece harpoon. Although we spent merely a month there, I grew to love—I don't think that's too strong a word—the people themselves.

I don't wish to sound sentimental, because the Far North is far more carnivorous than it is sentimental, but I found a steadiness and sureness about these people in northern Greenland that struck a deep chord in me. There is an acceptance of what *is* rather than, as we are prone to do here in the South, a steady grousing about what *should be*. If a blizzard catches you dogsledding alone dozens of miles out on the sea ice, you must accept that you can't push through it using just brute force and willfulness—our egotistical solutions here in the South. You must submit to the blizzard, summoning the patience and forbearance to sit quietly behind a chunk of ice, out of the wind. There you can rest with your head propped on your knees in the Eskimo style, perhaps for several days, as the blizzard rages around you; you must wait it out. What you need for this is humility and one hell of a lot of confidence.

Maybe that's what attracts me to these people, their sense of confidence in the face of difficulty. God knows, I could have used it at times in my life. They live each day with the knowledge that life is as full of risks as it is of the icebergs that stud their frozen seas, and that you maneuver among them as best you can. That shy, fearful boy that I had been didn't understand this metaphor. He knew the risks of snow and ice, he could live with them, and was confident among them, so that was the world he liked best. It was the world of people that troubled him. He wanted to know absolutely for sure about people but there is no sureness, just as there is no sureness among the icebergs. To him the risks with people looked dark, hidden, even malevolent; he couldn't understand them, and so he shied away.

As I grow older, the pattern begins to reverse: I feel less uncertainty toward the world of people and more toward snow and ice. I'm hardly old, barely forty, but I see that death has approached that much closer and my legs are that much stiffer. When I ski the backcountry chutes, I worry now in a way that I didn't when I was younger. I worry about falling and crashing into the rocks below. I worry that that steep slope of beautiful powder—the one that I would have skied so eagerly when I was younger—might break loose and bury me in a rumbling, icy avalanche.

If, as a young boy, I saw in the snow my father's face and my grandfather's in the ice, I now sometimes imagine the face of

God. I study a steep, beautiful, untracked powder slope, and its blank, white surface reveals nothing. I ask what this slope intends—what it *means*—and it doesn't answer. It could hold a wild, heart-pumping run through powder or a slow, suffocating death by burial. I won't know for sure exactly what it means until I ski it, and even then I may find that it means nothing more than it is, that, like God, it means whatever I want it to mean.

I still love winter and snow and ice—I love them more than I ever have—but I see them differently now. On their surface I've spread out the chaos that was once my life and assembled something that I hope approaches grace. To the boy that I was, snow and ice were a small, private world that made him feel big; to the man they are huge beyond reckoning and make him feel small. Now his sense of sureness resides in that very enormity and all-embracing power, and he gives himself over to snow and ice in a different, quieter way than did the small boy who loved to dive into the drifts.

I think to the North. I think of the whiteness that caps our planet and I think of it lowering to meet me as winter descends, as it did during that anxious October years ago. I see that the cold whiteness at the top of our planet is connected to the cold, infinite depths of space. I see it coming down and enveloping me and taking me up with it. I see in that whiteness both the soft comfort of death, and a thousand joyous ways to glide and to skate and to tumble and to roll, right through it.

The Way Down: Winter Sports

Leaps of Faith

The three ski jumps are strung across the face of a steep ridge in the Iron Range, a series of ore-veined hills that rise up like hard, knobby vertebrae from the frozen forests of Michigan's Upper Peninsula. Neatly lined up in order of size, the jumps, owned by the Ishpeming Ski Club, represent three rungs on a jumper's ladder to success.

The largest, its scaffold rising far above the ridgetop, is rated at 70 meters, which means that a jumper standing in the starting gate can usually plan on flying that far. Measured from the top of the scaffold to the bottom of the landing hill, it is as tall as a 34-story building. Its name is Suicide.

Next to it, with a slightly smaller scaffold, is the 50-meter hill, the one known as Homicide. Finally, down at the far end of the line and nearly hidden in the trees, is the 30-meter junior hill, a mere playground slide compared to the other two.

That's if you're looking at it from below. I, however, am standing on the starting platform of this third jump. The long ramp leading down from my skis ends abruptly at what looks to me like the South Rim of the Grand Canyon. My mentors, veteran jumpers, wait patiently on the canyon floor. They call this jump, which is often used by younger jumpers, Pesticide.

Up in the starting gate, I gather my nerve. The back of my brain tells me not to throw myself over the edge of the cliff. The front of my brain tells me that this sport might not conform to the laws of Newtonian physics. But one of my mentors has told me an old rule: "If you walk up that hill, you ride."

Don't get me wrong. I've skied steep stuff before—Elevator Shaft and Bear Paw at Aspen, the left chute at Tuckerman's Ravine, that sort of thing. And I don't mind catching a little air, like dropping off those big cornices we used to find at Loveland Pass. But this is different. This nordic ski jumping is to catching a little air what the cruise missile is to the crossbow.

It's like this: You clamp on a pair of fat, 250-centimeter-long skis that turn about as easily as a freight train and are equipped with cable bindings that permit the heels to lift freely and the jumper to lean forward. Then, balanced on these behemoths, you build up a head of steam by skiing straight down a long ramp. The ramp is as steep as the steepest black-diamond ski run, but unlike your average black-diamond run, this one ends in thin air.

Where the ramp ends, the fun begins. Howling along as you reach the edge, you are expected to *dive* over this precipice. *Headfirst*. And don't forget to keep those arms stylishly at your sides.

There's nothing frilly or baroque about it. You go straight, you go fast, and the snow, invariably, is rock-hard. The lingering impressions are of power, cold and metallic. Place names such as Ironwood, Iron Mountain, Copper Peak; the steel girders and frost-coated timbers that support the jump scaffolds; mercury-vapor lights and cinder-block warming huts; chain saws and snowmobiles; the frightening roar of wind and skis; the yellow stains the jumpers melt into the snow before they leave the top.

For decades, Ishpeming (pop. 7,500) has been a bastion of ski jumping. It is an iron-mining town. The old frame houses set against the hillsides are small, unpretentious, decidedly Midwestern. Not a lot of turbo-powered Saabs here—Ishpeming's streets rumble with big 4 x 4 pickups, "North Woods Cadillacs." And forget the Mexican beer and croissant sandwiches; this town celebrates its diverse ethnic heritage with items like pasties (a Cornish meat pie traditionally eaten by miners) and an esoteric sausage sandwich known as a "Cudighi" (COO-da-ghee). Wash it down with a Stroh's.

A chic resort it is not, but folks were jumping here and all over the Upper Peninsula long before anyone had heard of Aspen or Sun Valley. The sport arrived with Scandinavian immigrants, and Ishpeming held its first jumping tournament in 1888.

Since then, Ishpeming has produced something like a dozen national champions and Olympic contenders. The popularity of jumping has declined in Ishpeming and elsewhere in the Upper Peninsula in the last few decades, but the area is still dotted with jumping hills.

Even in its heyday, though, ski jumping probably wasn't a glamour sport, at least not around here, and certainly not in comparison to modern alpine skiing. Nor were the jumpers I met hot, young heroes bound for the Olympic training facility at Lake Placid. Most were veterans in their late twenties and thirties, many of them family men, postal clerks and pipe fitters who spend their weekends on the hill. Their glory is a home-grown sort, bestowed at tournaments where the announcers coin courageous nicknames (Black Hawk, the Green Hornet) while the fans, drinking beer and eating bratwurst, pound on their car horns to salute a fine jump or a spectacular recovery.

In a sense, ski jumping is a dinosaur of a sport, a throwback to some per-aerobic era when fans and athletes were simply in search of a thrill. One could even call it quaint, were it not for the raw, gritty power of jumper and jump.

There is absolutely nothing quaint about, say, the 120-meter "ski-flying" hill at the Upper Peninsula's Copper Peak, the largest jumping hill in the Western Hemisphere. From the top of its scaffold you can see into the next time zone. A skeletal steel structure, it projects from the hilltop like some ancient Mayan observatory, a place of secret and unspeakable rites. To visualize the landing hill that stretches below it, imagine two football fields, place them end to end, and tilt them at an angle approximating the steepest ski slope you've ever seen.

The landing hill at Copper Peak is serviced by a chairlift; at the top of the chair, a jumper enters an elevator that carries him close to the top of the scaffold. From there, he can see straight down through the metal-grate flooring to the hilltop, some 26 stories below. The jumper will be hurtling at more than 60 miles per hour on his way down those 26 stories. When he hits the takeoff, he'll have another 35 stories still to drop.

The record on the hill is 505 feet—in the air. Certainly not quaint. We're talking about industrial-strength sport.

Ski jumping is neither as dangerous nor as frightening as it might look (and it can look plenty frightening when you're standing at the starting platform). Nor is it as difficult to learn as one might think. It does, of course, take years of practice to be a *good* jumper, and there's no guarantee that you won't get hurt. But, with proper instruction, a competent alpine skier—or even a non-skier—should be able to handle the small hills in a fairly short time. One jumping coach tells of a 35-year-old non-skier who was riding a 40-meter hill after only two weeks of practice. Probably the most difficult thing for many would-be jumpers is simply finding a jumping hill in the first place.

I had no trouble finding them in the Upper Peninsula. I spent nearly a week there, starting my training at Ironwood, where the Wolverine Nordic Ski Club maintains several jumps just out of town ("Turn left at the oil tanks"). Club members outfitted me and coached me on the very small 10-meter hill. Then I drove to Ishpeming, about 140 miles away, where I practiced on the somewhat larger 15-meter hill. Finally, at Ishpeming, I worked up my nerve for the 30-meter hill, the one known as Pesticide.

The first thing you learn is that nordic jumping bears little resemblance to the casual jumps made by alpine skiers. The key to it all is aerodynamics. When a nordic jumper is stretched out headfirst in the air, his body and skis create an airfoil that, like an airplane wing, provides lift. Jumpers call this "riding the wind" and say it's the sport's ultimate thrill. Like the pilot of an airplane using ailerons, a jumper can correct his flight with slight movements of his hands, head, and shoulders. To this end, skiers have been known to suspend themselves in wind tunnels, experimenting with the body position that offers the most lift. Jumpers in Duluth, Minnesota, have ridden in a school bus cut open at both ends, cruising along at 60 miles per hour.

Attaining an aerodynamic form depends on a good takeoff. As he plunges down that long upper ramp (known as an inrun), the jumper adopts a low crouch. His chest is near his thighs, and his arms are straight behind him like the swept-back wings of a small jet winding up for takeoff. In a gathering roar he rushes toward the lip, skis rippling in the frozen ruts, wind lashing about his limbs—*whump*—then he shoots past, exploding from his crouch, launching kangaroolike over the edge. Then there is only the tear of the wind as he rips through the early-morning calm.

The move is difficult, powerful, and precise. Done correctly, it puts the jumper far forward over his skis. Some jumpers simply call their skis "the *big* boards." They weigh as much as 20 pounds per pair and can measure out at more than eight feet, compared to perhaps 10 pounds and seven feet for a big pair of alpine skis. They are cut with several grooves, have no metal edges, and are designed to provide speed and stability on the snow and to create a winglike surface in the air. "At 60 miles per hour, try holding an eight-foot plank out your car window and see how it handles," says John Kusz, a 34-year old Ironwood postal worker who holds the national veterans' distance record for 90-meter jumps (305 feet, but that doesn't count his ski flying at 120-meter Copper Peak).

It was the skis that worried me most. On my first day's practice, Kusz put me on a pair and sent me down Ironwood's landing hills. It suddenly became clear that jumping skis like to go very fast and very straight. They do not want to turn. But my real fear about these skis had to do with the tips. Alpine skiers frequently drop their ski tips while they're in the air and simply pull them back up before landing. But nordic jumping skis are so big, and present so much surface to the wind, that once the tips are down it's no easy matter to bring them back. Dropped tips can pull a jumper over forward into a serious nose dive. This is something you want to avoid.

There are ways. Jumpers must keep their legs straight. If a nordic jumper pulls his knees up like an alpine hotdogger, he is committing one of jumping's greatest sins—his ski tips will tend to drop. Likewise, a jumper must time his takeoff. On a big hill, he might be moving at 80 feet per second, and if he jumps too late, his ski tips may swing up too far; too early, and the opposite can happen—kiss those tips goodbye.

Once the jumper is past the lip, which slants slightly downward, his flight follows the curve of the carefully contoured landing hill. He's rarely more than 10 or 15 feet off the ground.

Proper style calls for a telemark landing. Assumed upon a jumper's return to Earth, it bears a curious resemblance to genuflection. This technique absorbs some of the impact. On the steep hill (35 to 39 degrees), the touchdown can be surprisingly gentle. This steep landing slope, in a sense, is the jumper's safety net. It presents no obstacles (like trees), its steepness cushions a fall, and its hard surface enables a falling skier to slide—rather than tumble—to a stop.

Jumpers insist on this hard surface; maintaining the jumping hill is a task that demands hours of sliding, scraping, and shoveling. At Ishpeming, for instance, I watched jumpers "snow" the scaffold of the 70 meter; in the course of two days they hoisted some 200 barrels of snow to the top of the scaffold, aided by a squeaky pulley and a pickup truck. At Ironwood, the jumpers sometimes hang on a rope over the landing hill—swinging like a pendulum—and pack the snow with their boots. The Ironwood jumpers, an imaginative lot, once held a beer party on an unpacked outrun, hoping to achieve the same effect.

It's nice to know a landing hill has been properly prepared. If a jumper flies beyond it, however, and lands where the slope flattens out, it doesn't much matter what landing style he adopts— he's going to come in like a ton of bricks.

This is called "outjumping" the hill, and it can result from an inrun that's too slick, allowing a jumper to build up too much speed. When this is a problem, jumpers can depart from a lower starting platform and watch where they land in relation to the red line that indicates the "K" point, the point where the landing hill begins to flatten. As John Kusz says, "If you see the red line go by, it's time to get concerned." In a sense, outjumping the hill is the equivalent of the test pilot's "edge of the envelope"—when you run out of hill, you run out of luck.

I was not about to run out of hill. I was having trouble enough with a 10-meter jump, a shamefully small bump my mentors called a "peewee" hill.

I'd spent my first day's practice at Ironwood, under the careful tutelage of John Kusz, skiing straight down the landing hill of a 50-meter jump. The next day I assaulted the 10-meter hill.

After a preliminary attempt that amounted to nothing more than a little hop, I decided on my second try that I'd really nail the thing, put some muscle into my takeoff and *dive* over that lip without a trace of fear.

I landed on my face. I planted it firmly in the snow between my skis and belly-flopped down the landing hill. I slid to a stop, gasping for breath. I felt like I'd been punched in the nose.

I picked myself up, pretending it was nothing. But from then on, the 30-meter hill—my goal—began to assume the proportions of the 120-meter monster over at Copper Peak. Riding Copper Peak was beyond the scope of my imagination, not to mention my abilities; a nose dive off a 30 meter was not.

My problems on the 10 meter aside, ski jumping looks more dangerous than it is, an image bolstered by those "agony of defeat" film clips, which, according to some jumping officials, have hurt the sport in this country more than anything else. "Safe," however, is a relative word in any sport, and in ski jumping, as in alpine skiing, there are the inevitable war stories.

Dale Fredette, for instance, president of the Ishpeming Ski Club and a veteran jumper, once tipped over in the air on a 50-meter hill, caught a ski tip, and was slapped to the ground, breaking four ribs and an ankle and rupturing his diaphragm. ("Oh, boy, did that hurt," says Fredette.) Also in Ishpeming, there's the story of three jumpers who broke their ankles using the same pair of skis. The owner of the skis, believing them jinxed, literally gave them the ax.

And over in Ironwood, Guy Orlich, a relative newcomer to

jumping, will tell you about the time he lost his skis in midair. Uninjured, he climbed back up the hill and was greeted by a pair of veterans singing a song to the effect, "Always check your bindings/Before you leave the top . . . "

The list could go on, but the truth is that crashes are not frequent; in the fifty or sixty jumps I witnessed, I don't remember a single fall other than my own. Like alpine skiing, the crashes that do occur don't usually result in injuries. When there are injuries, they are very rarely severe. According to at least one set of statistics, jumping is safer than alpine skiing. It's easy to forget jumping's built-in safety factors.

It's particularly easy to forget about them when you're standing at the top of that long, steep inrun. Even experienced jumpers admit to bouts of nervousness, especially on an unfamiliar hill, or on the first jump of the day when the snow conditions are unknown and a patch of sticky snow on the takeoff or landing could send a jumper tumbling headlong. "We call them moths," says one jumper. "They're bigger than butterflies."

It helps if you're younger. Ishpeming's Fredette, who coaches kids of all ages, says jumpers should start early in life, "before you have any real fears. Then it's progression from there—you go to larger and larger hills." Now 39 years old, Fredette started at age six and was jumping a 70-meter hill at age eleven.

Fredette also puts a premium on aggressiveness. If you're cautious and back off from the forward flight position, he says, the air will push you backward and you'll drop straight down. "You always have to attack the hill; you can never retreat from it." When Ironwood's Joe Jindrich charges out of the starting gate, he announces, "Baby, you're mine."

Ultimately, I didn't have much choice. I could never admit that I backed down from a hill called Pesticide.

On a dreary late afternoon in Ishpeming, the squeaky pulley finally lapses into silence. The job is done—the 70 meter is covered with snow. A few of the workers, including Fredette and Tom Sodergren, another veteran Ishpeming jumper, walk over to the outrun of the 30-meter hill.

I stand at the top, the inrun stretching steep and symmetrical below me, flattening as it approaches the lip. The two ruts lead straight down—you don't need a trail map. Without the pulley, the silence hangs over the wooden hollow like the calm before a storm.

I slip my toes into the metal binding brackets, hook the cables over my heels, and carefully clamp down the levers. ("Always check your bindings/Before you leave the top.") I meticulously wipe my foggy goggles on my shirttail, pull them over my head, and peer down the inrun. In the flat light, I can't seem to locate the end of the jump. I shout down, "Do all those pine boughs mark the lip?" The reply—that they do—floats up from the bottom of a deep canyon.

I run the motions through my mind, trying to remember Fredette's basic rules: "Head up, legs straight, your momentum should always be forward, never back. You always have to be aggressive—there are no old cautious ski jumpers."

Right . . . but what about my ski tips? Before climbing the hill, I'd asked Fredette how could I be *sure* they'd come up. He said something about cocking the ankles. Sodergren, meanwhile, asked my preference in flowers.

I slide into the starting position, both hands on the railings of

the little platform, my ski tips hanging out over the steep of the inrun. I suppose I'm as ready as I'll ever be. Even if I'm not, it's too late now. Once you climb the hill, you ride.

I take one last look and push off.

Baby, you're mine.

My skis clatter over the edge. I wrestle them into the two tracks and drop into a crouch—chest against thighs, arms straight behind. I plunge down the inrun.

Fast. The wind begins to beat around my ears.

Faster. The rippling of the skis climbs steadily in pitch.

Too fast. I'm rushing toward the festive little pine boughs marking the lip.

Way too fast.

Beyond the lip, I can see nothing but the wooded hillside across the hollow, that and a lot of thin air. *This* is suicide.

I try to stand up, but the inrun suddenly flattens and I'm shoved back down by compression. My knees, weak with fright and surprise at my speed, almost buckle.

I clutch—how do you get off this thing? But whoever designed the first ski jump knew what he was doing. There is only one exit ramp on a ski jump.

I'm at the pine boughs. I spring up; I have no other choice. Then, remarkably, my tips come up and the hill drops away. I'm standing nearly upright—a long way from the proper flight position—but I suddenly feel secure. The huge skis seem to provide a platform, and the wind seems to hold me in place. Besides, as Fredette says, "Nobody ever got hurt while they were in the air."

The flight only lasts an instant. My skis skim the steep of the landing hill and I touch down, hardly noticing the impact. I'm vaguely in the telemark position as I shoot down the rest of the landing hill and through the transition at the bottom. I snowplow down the long, narrow outrun that has been cut through a stand of brush on the valley floor. I punctuate my stop with a whoop.

Someone shouts out, "I'll bet you want to do it again." "Yeah," I yelled back. But I'm not so sure. It's fast—*way* too fast.

I didn't rest well that night, haunted by visions of inruns, and the next day, when I returned to the 30 meter, I braced myself for speed. This time, I was ready. This time, the thrill overtook the fear—I wanted more.

I managed to squeeze in a few more jumps before I had to leave. I was flying maybe 70 or 80 feet, getting a bit of a feel for the air, becoming more confident with each try. Then I began to think about those big rides, the flights of 300, 400, 500 feet. I wanted to ride the wind. At least I think I did. We'll see—this winter I may visit John Kusz again.

You'd think that ski jumping would be more popular than it is. According to one estimate, there are only about 200 serious ski jumpers in the country. Sports like hang gliding and skydiving have enjoyed a vogue. The attraction of these sports, it seems, is that of ski jumping—the thrill of an unencumbered ride through the air, no-frills flying.

In Ishpeming and elsewhere in the Upper Peninsula, ski jumping has been on the decline for the last few decades. "It used to be that every neighborhood had a little hill," says Ishpeming's Sodergren. But the sport demands long hours of practice and hill maintenance, and some jumpers say it's simply easier for kids to get into alpine skiing, snowmobiling, and video games. "The kids are too lazy," one former jumper told me. "Why walk when you can ride a lift?" If only they knew what they were missing.

On a still and cloudless January afternoon, I stand along the knoll of the Ironwood 50 meter watching Guy Orlich, far above me, prepare for another flight. A big and outgoing man, he wears an all-black jumping suit emblazoned, like the front of his pickup, with the works BLACK HAWK. A former alpine instructor, he has been jumping only a few years, but, as he told me over beer and burgers one night, he dreams of someday going to Yugoslavia, the home of his ancestors, and riding the ski-flying hill there. "That would be dying and going to heaven."

The late-afternoon sunlight sparkles in the frost-covered treetops, and from off in the distance drifts the faint howling of a pack of hounds hot on a rabbit's trail. Orlich, as he puts on his skis up above, breaks into song, and John Kusz responds with a clear, melodious yodel.

Then there's the slap of skis in the frozen ruts, the ripple and chatter and gathering rush, the *whump* as the jumper launches into the air.

Sliding to Glory

Steered true, a luge sled runs nearly silent, its journey down that twisting tube of ice accompanied by little more than the low whir of polished steel runners cutting cleanly across the sculpted surface at 50 or 60 or 70 miles per hour.

So when something goes wrong, you can hear it happen. Ten

feet up the wall on a big curve, a sled going out of control emits a wild shriek; those heavy, gleaming runners skid sideways across the curve's frozen face as sled and driver careen toward the wooden barrier that lines the top of the track. Steel ripping ice, that screech imparts a chill like fingernails on a blackboard. It is a sound I came to know and fear during the week I spent in Lake Placid, New York, learning how to luge.

You've seen luging—it appears on TV once every four years before dropping from sight until the next Winter Olympics. A derivation of nineteenth-century sled racing down the Alps' snow-covered roads, this is the sport in which the competitors lie flat on their backs on highly engineered 48-pound sleds and shoot down a tubular track trying to shave hundredths of a second from their times. This is the sport whose champions tend to speak in heavy Eastern European accents and look like something out of a bad sci-fi movie, dressed in shiny skin-tight suits, bubble-shaped visors, and pointy-toed booties. This is the sport in which I wanted to be a winner. Luging was almost unknown in this country, and I got the impression that it offered an easy way to the Olympics—or an easy way to die.

It is said that years ago, a luger simply had to show up in order to represent the United States in international competition. More recently, American youths seemed to stumble onto the sport and rise quickly through the ranks. In the late 1970s, for instance, high school student Frank Masley showed up in Lake Placid, and after a week and a half of training, went to Europe with the U.S. junior team. Now he's one of the top U.S. men's lugers. Likewise, as a California high school student, Bonny Warner won an essay contest sending her to Lake Placid to be a torchbearer for the 1980 Olympics. She heard about luging there and went to Europe to train using $5,000 she won in a Levi Strauss promotional drawing. Today she is one of the country's best woman lugers. Then there was George Tucker, a Puerto Rican citizen who grew up in Albany. He put together his own one-man luge team for the 1984 games at Sarajevo and became the first Puerto Rican Winter Olympic team in history.

After hearing enough stories like these, I finally had to try it. Last winter I showed up at Lake Placid equipped with elbow pads, running shoes, and visions of glory. Of course, I wasn't really expecting to make the Olympic team after a week's practice, but I figured *what the hell—you never know*. I'd once been pretty hot stuff on a Flexible Flyer; maybe the coaches would recognize my raw and untapped talents. And I figured it couldn't be too difficult to learn—certainly easier than ski jumping, which I had attempted the previous winter. As my friend Steve Krauzer pointed out before I left for Lake Placid, "How much training could you possibly need to be a human cannonball?"

There is no sign posted on the outskirts of Lake Placid proclaiming it "America's Sledding Capital," but there should be. It has the nation's only refrigerated bobsled run and its only full-scale luge course. It's the site of the North American championships for both toboggans and skeletons, one-man sleds that are ridden headfirst down the bob run.

The town is a curious mix of brick-and-clapboard New England village and metal-and-glass international sporting community. Among its winter sports facilities—most built for the 1932 and 1980 Winter Olympics—it counts ice rinks, ski areas, ski jumps, and several big frame boarding houses that cater to the intense young athletes who come for the winter, their rigorous schedules taken up with coaches and tutors.

On my first morning in town, I checked into the U.S. Luge Association's (USLA) offices in the Olympic Training Center on Main Street, a few steps down from the Ancient Mariner bar. I picked up my $25 luge association membership, which would give me access to equipment, the luge course, and coaching, and hitched a ride to the track with a vanful of lugers.

The sight did little for my confidence. Winding in serpentine coils down the forested slopes of Mount Van Hoevenberg, the luge course measures nearly two-thirds of a mile in length with a vertical drop of about 300 feet. It sports 12-foot-high walls on its bigger curves and is monitored by an elaborate system of control towers. Constructed of white concrete and lined with two inches of clear, refrigerated ice, the track, in all, represents a $6-million improvement on your local sledding hill.

I flashed my pass at the gate, crossed the footbridge over the bob course, and made my way up a snowpacked path alongside the luge course, past clusters of helmeted athletes in skintight suits. About a third of the way up the course, at Curve 10, I found Dmitry Feld, a 29-year-old Russian emigrant and former luger. Not long ago, he was teaching dog grooming at a school in Manhattan; now he's a USLA coach and manager of the U.S. Junior Team.

A luger (or "slider") came screaming through Curve 10, high on the wall. I introduced myself to Dmitry and asked him the procedure for beginners. "Go get sled and helmet," he said in heavily accented English, "and I show you how to steer. Then I bless you," he said, making a sign of the cross, "and off you go."

It took Dmitry about three minutes to explain the fundamentals of luging to our small group of beginners. Riding a luge has been compared to riding a bar of soap, but technically speaking, steering one is no more difficult than steering a bicycle. To go left, you push down against the sled with your left shoulder and push in against the right runner with your right foot. The motion is actually a lot like rolling out of bed. What is difficult is steering the proper amount at the proper points. As "Bullet Bob" Hughes, another luge coach, says, "Each curve of the track has its own program."

A poorly steered sled loses time by skidding on curves and slamming into the walls of straightaways—easy to do when you're threading the needle down those four-foot-wide chutes at 50 or 60 miles per hour. Even without mishaps, taking a poor line—climbing too high on a curve, for instance—can cost dearly in a sport where times are computed to the thousandths of a second.

As in auto racing, the faster you go, the more precise your timing and steering must be. A luger who has departed from the men's start at the very top of the Lake Placid course (luge courses have several starting points) will average a curve every three seconds, hit speeds approaching 70 miles per hour, and undergo such centrifugal force through the big curves that he'll wear a neck strap (attached to a chest harness) to prevent his head from being pulled down against the ice. From the top, the slider must also deal with tricky spots like the one between Curves 2 and 3, where the proper line is described as a "window" by one luger. "Either you're in it," he says, "or you hit the sill."

It's a sport where you want to sleep well the night before; besides quick reactions, you need the ability to remain relaxed. *Stay calm* when you see that big curved wall approaching. If you get anxious and tense up, or try to lift your head and shoulders for a better view, the sled, suddenly destabilized, might begin to skid. *Keep cool* when you're about to slam the wall of that straight. If you don't, your ride might end with the announcer's amplified epitaph, "Eighty-one at 13." Translated, this means that at Curve 13 the sled is without a slider.

Walkie-talkie in hand, Dmitry climbed onto a low stretch of wall to watch the more advanced sliders come down, one after the other arcing high and fast across the big white face of Curve 10, some shooting up toward the wooden barrier with a screech.

This is where we'd begin. Our first runs would take us from Curve 10 through the lower third of the course. ("It's very slow," Dmitry reassured us.) Then we would work our way up to Curve 9, then 8, then 7, and on up the track.

At Curve 10 my colleagues included Dave, 21, a part-time community college student from Buffalo; Anne, a 31-year-old consultant for a communications firm; and 13-year-old Gordy, from the New York City area, who was spending much of the winter at Lake Placid. One of our number, Peter "They call me Merv" Brisbois, sported a ponytail, Vuarnets, and camouflaged tennis shoes. He came from Santa Cruz, was into "downhill skateboarding" (he was once clocked at 72 mph), and, as another luger skidded wildly through Curve 10, very sensibly asked Dmitry to tell us how to avoid "the big crash."

Four of the group were British. Already experienced, they were here to learn the course for an upcoming international junior race; one of them, 18-year-old Nick Ovett, was the brother of runner Steve Ovett, Olympic gold medalist in the 800 meters at Moscow.

The announcer gave the two-minute warning for spectators to vacate the area around Curve 10.

"It will just *explode* in front of you," one Brit told me.

"All this white," said another.

"You'll have a real buzz when you get to the bottom," said the first.

"See you in London," said Dmitry, sending a British sled on its way down the track.

I was the last to go. Dmitry gave me a little shove, sending me trundling toward Curve 10. I felt like I'd been strapped into one of those reclining lawn chairs, the kind on wheels, and it was about to roll down a very large hill.

Gravity slowly began to show its stuff. The sled rumbled through Curve 10, picking up a little speed. Into 11, faster now, climbing a little up the wall, tilting to the right through the long tunnel of white ice, faster. I suddenly felt locked into a groove, helpless without brakes, no sense of steering, no way out of this ice-coated drainpipe, no choices at all.

Curve 12, a flip to the left, Curve 13, a flip to the right, the course coming at me faster and faster like some surreal art movie, all white and twisty and tunnel-like. Relax, give yourself over to it. Curve 14, a long ride with my head bouncing up and down like a rag doll as the sled hit small bumps, then a quick flip through 15, and I was into the loose snow of the finish chute, exhilarated.

Bullet Bob, standing on the wall and gnawing on a lunchtime drumstick, said it was one of the better first runs he had seen lately.

After dinner that first night I retired for a beer to the dim warmth of the Mariner, noticing several large and slightly ominous-looking men sitting at the bar. I didn't know what they were speaking, but it wasn't English. Skeleton riders, probably.

My other two runs that first day hadn't gone as well as the first. On my second run I had banged into the wall at least twice between Curves 12 and 13, a sensation comparable to getting slammed into the boards by a hulk of a defenseman during a high school hockey game. On my third run I had discovered that the sled's steering did in fact work; I turned too early on 12, climbed the curve too high and too fast, and skidded down to slam the inside wall. Bullet Bob had said I was way too stiff; I should relax.

Sitting in the Mariner, reflecting on the day, I was surprised by luging's difficulty; even more surprising, however, was all the *ambition* I sensed. Besides the national team, which was in Europe, some sixty or seventy dedicated young lugers were spending the winter at Lake Placid and it seemed that most of them, including at least some of the rank beginners, were hoping for a trip to Calgary in 1988. "What are your aspirations?" I asked one luger. "What are anybody's?" came the reply.

It may have once been a relatively easy way to the Olympics, but these days luging in the United States is highly competitive. U.S. performance against the tough Europeans has improved, and interest has grown steadily since the 1980 Olympics at Lake Placid, with the real surge coming in the wake of the Sarajevo games. The USLA's membership now stands at about 700, up from less than 100 five or six years ago, and luging officials talk about restricting the increasingly crowded Lake Placid track to serious competitors. Meanwhile, luging has become a hot sport in certain other cold regions with new, shorter tracks at Marquette and Muskegon, Michigan, and Fairbanks, Alaska, in addition to the full-scale track under construction for the Calgary Olympics.

I mulled this all over at the Mariner, saddened that the games were forever out of reach, while the big guys across the bar spoke softly in strange tongues.

Skeleton riding, *yes*. Now there's a *truly* obscure sport, like U.S. luging 15 or 20 years ago.

It amounts to belly-flopping onto a 100-pound cafeteria tray equipped with stainless steel runners and riding it headfirst down the bobsled course at speeds approaching 80 miles per hour. Skeletons don't round some curves so much as ricochet off them, and when a rider brushes up against rough spots in the walls, one tells me, "you can smell your nylon suit burning."

"Our viewpoint on skeletons is this," said Bullet Bob: "If you crash, would you rather hit your head or your feet?"

I knew that the U.S. Skeleton Association had about twenty members, only twelve of them active, five of them on the national team. There was hope after all. I pictured myself sauntering through the snowpacked streets of St. Moritz wearing one of those dark blue parkas with the big white letters on the back— USA SKELETON.

But not this year. I couldn't quit luging while still at Curve 10. Besides, I'd heard there'd be a master's race that weekend for the over-30 set. It would be conducted from the women's start, about three-quarters of the way up the course. To hell with Calgary, I decided, ordering another beer. I just wanted to compete in that old-guy's meet.

Bundled in parka and big boots against a bitter wind, Dmitry paced slowly back and forth on top of a low stretch of wall below Curve 13, remarking that the weather reminded him of his Russian army stint "at China border." I'd joined him after my day's practice—having worked my way up a few curves higher on the course—to watch the more advanced lugers negotiate a particularly difficult section between 12 and 13. Its centerpiece was a short, tough straight known as the "Hogpen," where, according to the prevailing track wisdom, "the Grim Reaper waits."

Some of the riders took a beautiful line, sleds emitting that whir as they flashed past us. Others reminded me of the opening moments of a pinball game—the long, graceful arc of the sled swooping through horseshoe-shaped Curve 11—and then *ping, ping, ping zzzzzzzzttttt*, as sled and driver, misjudging 12, smashed from wall to wall through the Hogpen, finally losing it in a shriek and cloud of ice shavings, the luger coming around 13 sledless and on his back.

"In the beginning it's fun," Dmitry said philosophically, carefully appraising each run. "Then later, when you go up and up the track, it's not so fun—you take bad beatings. But then you start cooking, and it's the biggest fun. It's like you go in Audi 4000"— he grabbed an imaginary steering wheel and stomped down on an imaginary accelerator—"*zzzooommm*."

Lugers do take bad beatings. Serious injuries, according to one coach, are no more frequent in luging than in recreational skiing, but lugers suffer many more minor injuries than skiers—such as the bruises and contusions resulting from the impact of soft flesh on hard ice. Summer training, on wheeled sleds, poses other hazards. One luger told me about a very fast wooden track in Czechoslovakia that sent him to the hospital three times in three months to have splinters removed.

In spite of all this and in spite of the speed, Bullet Bob, who showed up in Lake Placid in 1976 when he was 21 and looking for excitement, drew parallels between luging and, of all things, golf. "It's a very intense mental sport," he said. "It requires great concentration. You might be facing wind, snow, cold, a fast course, but you have to be calm, collected. You can't get excited."

As former manager of U.S. teams touring Europe, including the 1984 Olympic team, Bob, now the USLA's resource development director, had seen a lot of luge courses. He described the Lake Placid track as the "Jekyll and Hyde course of luging—it has a fairly easy women's start, but an extremely testing men's start." The men's start house, he said, is often called "the morgue." The lugers waiting their turns there are very quiet.

On Friday, my fourth day of luging, I was given permission to advance to the women's start. This was a victory of sorts—now I could enter the weekend race. For the time being, however, the coaches still required me to brake—drag my feet and pull up on the sled—until I was a short way down the track, and I was still on a training sled that was considerably slower than the high-performance racing sleds. In the last few days I'd also done my share of rooting around in the Hogpen.

I met more sliders as I hung around the women's start house, also known as "the zoo," a dim, crowded, concrete-floored hut that, unlike the men's start house, had some of the sociable atmosphere of a summer camp.

Many of the sliders, I discovered, had other sorts of athletic backgrounds and had somehow learned about luge.

I met a gymnast, a swimming coach, a pilot, and, in Thorne Butler, 25, a former ski racer who ran a San Diego diving school. He came to Lake Placid on a $100 bet made while watching the Sarajevo Olympics with a friend. Jotham Stein, a self-described world traveler, rowed at Princeton, while Caroline Paul rowed for Stanford; Linda Livingston, a student at the University of Oregon, was an accomplished skydiver. These last two counted themselves among the "slam sisters," a group claiming an affinity for the walls.

Yet of all the lugers I met, I felt spiritually closest to 39-year-old Tom Thee, who every morning drove a vanful of lugers, myself among them, from the Olympic Training Center to the track. A log-home contractor from Anchorage, Thee was spending the winter at Lake Placid with his 16-year-old son, Shannon. "I want to do doubles with my kid," he said, referring to the event where two sliders pile onto one sled, "a father-son team—what do you think?" Thee said he'd be 42 for the 1988 Olympics, but pointed to the successes of older race-car drivers. "I'm dreaming a lot," he said, "but you never know."

I was dreaming a lot, too. It was from Thee that I learned the upcoming event was not some run-of-the-mill weekend master's race. This race, to my complete surprise, constituted the U.S. master's *nationals*. Finally, I'd have my shot at luging glory.

On Saturday morning, race day, I noticed a lot fewer sweatpants and sneakers and a lot more aerodynamic rubberized speed suits and streamlined vinyl booties, designed to pare fractions of a second from your time. The women's start house appeared more tense and crowded than usual.

Poised on the hut's wooden benches (one of them bearing a bumper sticker reading SCHOOL'S OPEN—DRIVE CAREFULLY), some of the sliders talked, some tinkered with their equipment, and some leaned back with eyes closed, moving head and shoulders this way and that as if in a fever dream. The decibel level rose and someone shouted, "Quiet."

My competition, as near as I could see among all the youth, consisted of at least one former national team member, several unknowns, and regulars like Tom Thee and Bill Horn. Wearing a bright blue speed suit and white booties, Horn, at age 65, was by far the oldest of the group, having taken up luge three years earlier when he retired from the Bell System and moved to the Lake Placid area. Horn had marketing experience and volunteered to raise funds for the luging program. "I just felt I could be a little more authentic dealing in the subject if I could slide," he said, "so I got on a training sled." He had since become an accomplished luger as well as something of a psych-out artist ("that bump down there in 5, did you notice that?")

Horn was one of the first to go. He exited to a chorus of "good luck, Bill." I continued with my preparations, donning the tight-fitting training suit I'd borrowed and coating my bubble-shaped face visor, also on loan, with Body on Tap, a type of shampoo that for some reason prevents fogging and is a fast-moving item at Lake Placid drugstores.

One by one the lugers left. Outside, the starting officials moved among the rows of sleds carrying some sort of electronic thermometer (heated runners are very fast and highly illegal). I was still on a trainer, however, and my runners were flecked with rust. No matter. My sled might be slow, but my competitors were few. To do well, maybe even cop a national master's ranking, I figured I simply had to complete all four runs. According to the rules, I would only have to cross the finish line four times in contact with my sled. I didn't even have to be *on* the sled.

My turn came up. I climbed aboard my sled, positioned on a flat square of ice at the top of the women's starting ramp, and pulled down on my visor, pretending I was closing the canopy of a small jet fighter. I could hear my labored breathing inside the clear plastic bubble—the "Darth Vader effect," one luger called it—as I waited for the light to turn green.

"Clear the track to the ladies' start," announced the loud-speaker.

"Track is clear to the ladies' start," it answered itself.

"Sled on the track," said the loudspeaker.

"Don't blow it, pal," I told myself.

Curve 4 came first. Lie back and get settled. Into 5, some speed now, steering with left foot and right shoulder, keeping it low. Out of 5 and under the footbridge, spectators' heads flashed past. Dmitry was here somewhere. Into the Labyrinth, a long, nearly straight stretch broken by four quick turns, four twists of the shoulders—6, 7, 8, 9—while the sled gathered speed with a low rumble rising in pitch, the sound of a bowling ball approaching the pins. The big white wall of Curve 10 loomed larger and larger as if I were seeing it through a zooming camera lens.

Wham, the world turned sideways to the left. Halfway up the wall, centrifugal force pushed body into sled, and sled into verti-cal ice, pulling my bouncing head down toward the track. *Wham*, the camera flipped all the way to the right as I entered Curve 11—Omega—a seemingly endless ride down a dim, curving tun-nel, its roof formed by canvas sunscreens. I had to steer to keep low, the sled swaying, cranking it over hard when I saw the tun-nel's end.

Through the little straight to 12, past the blue flash of Bullet Bob's parka, pausing on the way into 12, easing it up the wall. Steer hard *now*. Too late. I shot down off 12 and slammed into the wall of the Hogpen, the sled bouncing off, screeching briefly, and straightening out. A quick steer through 13, and down the straight toward 14, where I hit it right and began to hear the whir. Through the long, curving tunnel of 14, past the timer, through 15, and I plowed into the loose snow of the finish chute, pulling to a stop near the scales and officials who would weigh me and my sled to made sure I hadn't added illegal weight.

One down, three to go.

Late Sunday afternoon, Tom Thee's crowded van pulled into the darkening parking lot of Lake Placid's Olympic Training Center. Gingerly, I hobbled out and limped toward the light and warmth. A week's worth of wall-slamming had finally caught up with me. I felt like a fragile old man.

In the past two days, in both race runs and training runs, I had nearly clipped off Dmitry's boot toes when I slammed a wall at his feet. I'd frightened myself with a wild, looping ride through 12, the sled skidding uncontrollably up and down the wall, and at various points along the way, I'd thoroughly battered my shoulders and somehow crunched my foot.

But I'd had some good runs too, and, as I limped swiftly across the parking lot toward the master's awards ceremony, I relished my racing results. I had completed all four runs of the master's race, and had managed to break the top ten. I'd ended up seventh. In the *nation*.

So what if there were only eight entrants in the race, and one of them dropped out? Who cares that the winning times were in the 40- and 41-second range, while my best run was 48? And it didn't bother me that I had been trounced by a man 35 years my senior, Bill Horn, who finished third. These details were not troubling. When I saw the final standings, the fact remained. I was a champ.

Fear of Falling

At 4 A.M., mere hours before my run down Aspen's World Cup downhill course, I could have used a little of Giorgio Piantanida's enthusiasm for hazardous sport. During the winter, the big 19-year-old skis for the Italian downhill team. In the summer, he lives for motocross and American-style football: He plays a 97-kilo (213-pound) tight end for

The Frogs, a team outside Milan. When I met Giorgio in Aspen for the race, he was overflowing with exuberance—for the town, for the Los Angeles Raiders, and especially for downhill—which he expressed in two simple words: "Ees fhan-TAH-steec!"

While Giorgio wrestled with the language barrier, I wrestled with the specter of Aztec. It had been keeping me awake for weeks. Located halfway down the mountain, Aztec is a clifflike drop-off that is groomed glass smooth, then blasted in spots with giant blowtorches to harden the snow. Inching over the patches of ice, an expert recreational skier might make thirty turns to get down Aztec; a World Cup downhiller does it in three.

But Aztec is just the beginning. After plunging down its slippery face—freefalling toward the shimmering city of Aspen far below at 60...65...70...nearly 75 miles per hour—you suddenly swoop to the right, then rip to the left through a 90-degree cranker, known affectionately as the airplane turn, which happens to skirt the edge of a deep gulley. Not to worry. To snag errant downhillers, thoughtful race organizers have erected at 15-foot-high net, anchored with steel cables. They call it the Berlin Wall.

Oh, I liked the upper half of the course just fine. A rolling, mile-long ridgetop, it was as wide, as sunny, and as gentle as a golf fairway. With the psychic clarity acquired by hours of tossing and turning, I began to imagine it as a sort of high-mountain world of innocence and light. But all this was like the Sirens singing from the rocks, luring me down toward the dark, icy underworld whose portal would be Aztec.

I had other worries, too. Some were comparatively small matters: How far should I crank my bindings for those speeds and torques? Some were medium-sized: How can I slow myself on the steeps? And some were large: Am I a fool?

I was, after all, due to get married in a few weeks. Up on the mountain I'd been meeting racers who'd survived broken backs, shattered bones, blown-out knees. A fall at those speeds can be an ugly sight—a body cartwheeling down at 65 mph, bouncing on its head . . . its feet . . . its head . . . its feet . . . slinging off bits of equipment—poles, gloves, goggles—while two skis arch skyward as if launched from a bow. At 4 A.M. you can only hope its not you.

In more ways than one I was skiing from a good dream into a bad one. This was the World Cup circuit, the big time, the source of my daydreams nearly 20 years ago when I was a high school racer. Downhills in the Midwest, of course, amounted to about three turns and 30 seconds down a glorified cow pasture, followed by a sack lunch in the lodge. But I used to daydream a lot, about slopes spread with thousands of cowbell-ringing, wildly cheering fans, about dashing heroes like Jean Claude Killy roaring down breathtaking courses, about fur-draped women waiting at the finish.

I raced for a while in college, fell a lot, figured I'd smartened up, and finally hung it up. Then a few years ago, just for fun, I took up masters racing. I wrote a few things about skiing. And one day it dawned on me—maybe I could try Aspen.

Hyped as "America's Downhill," the Subaru Aspen Winternational World Cup is the biggest annual ski race in the United States, and one of the top ten downhills in the world. Since the first race there in 1981, Aspen has become a major stop on the World Cup circuit—the White Circus—a globe-trotting tour from the Alps to the Rockies, with occasional stops in the Andes, Scandinavia, Eastern Europe, and Japan. Most national teams spend nine months of the year on snow. For the U.S team, the season opens with training camps at Oregon's Mount Bachelor in May, moves to the Andes in midsummer, and ends on the glaciers of Switzerland and Austria in the fall.

Through the winter, the pace is relentless—a race each weekend, the skiers rising and falling in the standings, carrying with them, some would have us believe, the fortunes of nations. There is no love lost, particularly between the Swiss and the Austrians, countrymen whose national pride is so tied to ski racing that after some poor performances last year, the Austrian team is said to have received death threats.

The Austrians are especially serious about downhill: Slalom and giant slalom are events; downhill is a cult. Its mystique grows from its mountain-sized scale, thundering speeds, and wildly changing terrain—launching the racer into the air, squashing him into the snow, sucking him toward the fences. And where slalom and GS lean hard on technique, downhill also demands iron nerves. At Austria's infamous Hahnenkamm, in Kitzbühel, the pitches are so steep, so bumpy, and so icy that a racer trying to turn skips down them sideways at 70 mph, touching down every few yards with skis flapping about like a wash line in a hurricane. Says one American downhiller: "You're skipping and just going like a bat out of hell and you're just trying to keep things going in the right direction."

Downhillers, some say, are of a type: outgoing, swaggering, possessed of healthy egos. "They think they're big heroes," says Austrian team coach Dieter Bartsch. "They have to or they won't take the risks to the maximum."

Whatever it was, I was pretty sure I didn't have it. Maybe I never had, or maybe I'd lost it years ago. That brash, adolescent confidence drifts away; you get older and you worry more about some high-speed mistake sending you into the woods. Besides, I had marriage to think about. Physically, these guys were sleek and hard and full of fire; my life, in contrast, had softened and spread out to embrace responsibility and my wife-to-be, not to mention some major household appliances.

It was the difference between myself and my beefy friend Giorgio.

"The more fast," he informed me, "the more good."

At seven o'clock Tuesday evening, the skies above Aspen ripped open with chrysanthemum bursts of fireworks. Scores of skiers bore torches down the lower flanks of Aspen Mountain, weaving and bobbing like a swarm of fireflies, while downtown in Wagner Park, a crowd gathered around a giant bonfire. The fireworks boomed, the bonfire blazed, and the speakers pounded out rock n' roll: "I can feel it coming in the air tonight. . . . "

"Aspen very good city," said Giorgio. "All the time—in the morning, in the night. *Very* fun."

This year, though, everything had to be perfect. Last year's Aspen Winternational, as the weeklong celebration is known, was marred by a racers' boycott of the giant slalom, held the day after the downhill. Despite officials' attempts to go ahead with the event, the racers, claiming the snow was too soft from the previous night's rain, blockaded the course, canceling the race and ABC's big-ticket coverage of it. They also set off some dire speculation about the future of the World Cup now that "labor disputes" had entered the picture. Little old Aspen, meanwhile, felt kicked in the teeth by its guests.

Another unfortunate incident also occurred in 1986 when Swiss ace Peter Mueller, winning the Aspen downhill for the fourth time, refused, along with the two runners-up, to wear his number bib on the awards stand. SUBARU appeared on the bibs, and Mueller had asked for $5,000 to wear it. The Aspen Skiing Company, Subaru, The North Face, and other sponsors, by the way, shell out about $1 million for the event; a champion racer such as Mueller can earn about $500,000 a year by using certain manufacturers' products.

The main question this year, however, was which Swiss would win. Two Swiss skiers—Mueller and Pirmin Zurbriggen—were dueling it out for the World Cup overall downhill title. They'd been cleaning up all season, trashing archrival Austria. At 29, Mueller is an old man on the circuit, and consistently one of its top downhillers, but he had never won the overall title. He needed the Aspen victory to keep his hopes alive, for well ahead of him in the season's standings was Zurbriggen, five years his junior. Zurbriggen had recently shot to the top of the World Cup, racking up win after win in several disciplines, and some observers had begun comparing his versatility to that of Jean Claude Killy, who won all three men's alpine gold medals in the 1968 Olympics.

Mueller and Zurbriggen presented a contrast in personality as well: Mueller is big, ruddy-faced, and outspoken, while the slender Zurbriggen is described as soft-spoken and deeply religious. At Aspen, Mueller complained loudly about the course, about this year's tighter turns and slower speeds. "It is too bad they changed this from a real downhill," he said. Zurbriggen, a fine technician, found it to his liking. "Between me and Mueller it's an old fight," he noted, "but the course turns a little bit more, and that's good for me."

The Swiss held six of the coveted fifteen top-seed starting

positions, the beleaguered Austrians four, and the Italians two. Luxembourg, the United States, and Canada claimed one each. Olympic gold medalist Bill "Bad Boy" Johnson, who won the Aspen downhill in 1984, was out for the season with knee and back injuries. America's hopes rode with Doug Lewis, a 23-year-old from Salisbury, Vermont.

My own hopes rode with the race officials, who had questions—questions concerning skiing ability, injuries, image. Who could blame them? "We're trying to put on a world-caliber ski race," said one. "No offense to you, but how's it going to look if some bozo comes skiing down first?"

No, I wasn't exactly first-seed material, but I sure as hell didn't want to go at the tail end of the pack. After seventy or eighty racers, a course tends to look like a bad road in Baja, eroded with ruts, grooves, washboard. There was, however, an alternative to running last.

By rule, the first competitor in a race is preceded by several forerunners whose duty is to ensure that the timing system works, that the course is in order, and that the snow is well groomed. Sort of like guinea pigs. Also by rule, the race itself is preceded by several days of training runs. According to the week's minute-by-minute schedule, at precisely 10:17 A.M. on the first day of training, a special forerunner would leave the starting gate. That would be me—the first skier down the course for the 1987 Aspen Winternational.

"If you're afraid, you're not going to be a world-class skier," Doug Lewis told me as we rode up the Ruthie's Run chair lift. "If you hold back, you're probably going to get hurt."

I'd been cornering every racer I could and asking about how

they dealt with fear. Actually, what I really wanted to know was how *I* should deal with fear.

Almost everyone emphasized one thing: Whatever you do, don't panic. When in trouble or frightened, a skier tends to lean back, open up. But say you hit a big bump while sitting back like that. Your skis will shoot skyward, your head will drop back, and suddenly you're flying along upside down at 60 mph wondering how you'll feel when you land. That'll give you something to panic about. The coaches have a solution to this: "Attack."

Doug Lewis had additional advice. "Stay balanced," he said. "If you're balanced, you can ride anything out; if you're not, you're history. And look ahead. You can't think about what you're doing now. You've got to be thinking about what's coming up, because by the time you think about it, you're past it."

Lewis used to push his limits a little too hard, as many young downhillers do. "Then they usually go through a crash," he said, "and that smartens them up." His own smartening up occurred during the 1981 Aspen downhill, in the form of tower number eight of the chair lift we were sitting on. He slammed into it, broke his back, and spent the next three months in a corset.

Lewis, who had just placed seventh in the recent downhill in Furano, Japan, was the top-seeded U.S. downhiller. America has never been a downhill power like, say, Austria. It wasn't until 1984 that an American male, Bill Johnson, won a World Cup and captured a gold medal in the Olympics. One reason, say U.S. Ski Team officials, is that liability problems make it difficult to ski fast on U.S. mountains.

Young Europeans, in contrast, get a lot more training at speed. U.S. men's downhill coach Theo Nadig described returning to his hometown in Switzerland and skiing for an afternoon with a bunch of 9- and 10-year olds. "I mean, they ski like crazy," he said. "They tuck, they jump . . . and maybe once in a while they run someone over, but there is not a lawsuit or anything. They just go . . . they're used to speed."

Going fast, though, isn't simply a matter of "pointing 'em straight." On flat sections of a course, the racer must squeeze speed from his skis by staying as low as possible in his tuck, and by keeping his skis absolutely flat. You know they're flat when your skis weave drunkenly together and apart. (I began thinking of this phenomenon, which I desperately wished to avoid, as The Big Swim.) Nor is holding a tuck as simple as it looks. Try squatting for two or three minutes with chest against thighs, shins vertical and thighs horizontal. Most mortals will feel like the electric coils from a toaster oven have been embedded in their quads. Then, to reproduce the "squash" of a deep compression in the course, ask somebody to jump on your back.

"Line" is the thing here; as opposed to, say, driving a car down a narrow highway, downhill more closely resembles maneuvering a kayak through churning rapids, avoiding rocks and holes, seeking the deepest, fastest water. Between gates that often are spaced hundreds of yards apart, a racer skis where he wishes. He can traverse uphill to set up, drop down to gain speed, ski around a bump or over it, carve rounded turns or sharp ones. It's often the case, however, that the fastest line is also the riskiest line.

It's here, beyond pure technique, that the sport of downhill enters the shadowy realm of psychology. For instance, on the Steilhang, a precipitous headwall of the Hahnenkamm, the fastest line nearly clips the nets. Says Austrian coach Bartsch: "You have to be so confident you're going to make it." Likewise on the course at Val Gardena, Italy. There lie the infamous Camel

Bumps, the three consecutive bumps where Johnson lost it last year. You can safely ride over each one, or take a chance and leap from the second to the third, flying as high as 25 feet off the ground. You stand to gain a little time by jumping, but, as U.S. downhiller Mike Brown cautions, "if you miss your jump, you're probably hatin' life."

Brown, wearing eight screws in his left hand from a recent fall, describes a "little rise" that a downhiller must make: "from the fear that 80 miles per hour is too fast, to the fear that 80's not fast enough."

I was nowhere near Brown's "little rise."

In fact, I was probably backing away. As part of my "training" for Aspen, I'd skied downhills at Big Sky and Big Mountain, Montana, joining dozens of fast, fearless adolescents with pimples and skintight suits. (The word on the slopes was "skin to win.") At Big Sky, I also ran a super G, a hybrid of downhill and giant slalom. Coming out of a fast turn and trying to go faster, my skis split apart, tripping me like a log trips a runner, and I launched into a long dive that ended with a face plant. The momentum carried me cartwheeling down a steep headwall, and I got my smartening up. The impact bent a ski, bruised my confidence, and snapped an eyetooth.

As the week went on, small jets winged into the airport, disgorging revelers. By day, Aspen's wide streets and tasteful pedestrian malls were wreathed in clouds of dust, sun, and mink. The scent of Yves Saint Laurent perfume and mesquite-grilled chicken clogged the air. Tanned, slim, exuding an aura of hip wealth and athleticism, the afternoon crowd lounged in sunglassed splendor on the deck at Little Nell's, the Police wailing from outdoor speakers: "RRROXXanne, you don't have to wear that dress tonight. . . ."

By night, you could cruise down to The Paradise and take in the Nitty Gritty Dirt Band, or truck out to Snowmass for a black-tie dinner-dance for charity (tickets $250 and up). For considerably more cash, you could sip champagne in the heavily draped drawing rooms of the Jerome, Aspen's grand old Gilded Age hotel, and purchase one of the celebrity-laden ski teams—whose members included John Denver, Billy Kidd, Leon Uris, Barbi Benton, and friends—auctioned off in a Calcutta pool to benefit the U.S. Ski Team.

But the best and probably most exclusive hangout in town was the basement of the Continental Inn, the hotel where the racers stayed. On lazy afternoons, as temperatures hit 60 under a blinding sun, you could enter a dank, dripping garage tunnel and, with the right credentials, walk into a cool, flourescent-lit netherworld of activity.

It was here that the technicians had set up shop. The basement had been partitioned into two dozen plywood cubicles, each occupied by a ski manufacturer and crammed with work benches, tools, and skis, and guarded by padlock. ("We're onto some good things here," one technician explained. "No reason to share them.") Amid the smell of melting wax and the sounds of rasping files and foreign tongues, technicians hunched over timing charts—analyzing whose skis were running fastest on which part of the course—and labored over plastic bases and steel edges, coaxing a little more speed from those big, hand-built 225-centimeter-long boards.

Certain pairs of downhill skis, even from the same company,

seem to run faster than others. ("If you knew the reason," said one technician, "you'd be a rich guy.") A fast pair of downhill skis is handled like a Ming vase—unwrapped only for that single run on race day, treasured for years until passed down to a lucky young racer. For instance, a legendary pair named Speedy was built in the mid-seventies, spent years with the Swiss women's team, and was then acquired in 1983 by Canadian downhiller Laurie Graham. Weakened by years of filing, a ski edge ripped out during the 1987 Vail downhill (the women's counterpart to the Aspen race), and Graham finally laid Speedy to rest.

Even a fast pair of skis, however, must be perfectly prepared, its edges honed to precise bevels, its bases inscribed with tiny suction-breaking grooves and coated with mysterious wax combinations, scraped to a very fine film "thin to win." Technicians for top racers carry several extra pairs of skis to the start, each waxed differently in case, say, the sun disappears behind clouds. The technician buries the skis in the snow to cool them. And if I accidentally stepped on a pair when I was tromping around up there?

"They'd *kill* you," said one technician.

As the first training run approached, it seemed just about everyone in town was concentrating on how to go faster. In the basement, technicians filed and waxed; up on the mountain, competitors studied their lines; in the motel rooms, coaches discussed strategy; in the bars, revelers downed another round.

Everyone wanted to go faster except me. My main concern was still how to slow down. I figured I could control my speed by standing higher and making wider turns. This would work, I guessed, in all but one place: the lower half of Aztec—almost a straight shot—where racers have been known to hit close to 80 miles per hour. I'd have to follow it straight down, and hope body and soul held together at warp speed.

"Ten minutes," called a starting official.

All movement along the course ceased. Everyone was in position.

I waited, weak-kneed, in the sunny, fenced-in starting area, watching racers around me stretch their muscles, gather their wits, visualize their winning lines, while I prayed for one somewhere between total embarrassment and serious injury.

Helmets were scattered about the start. Ski techs carefully sifted snow over their precious stock. Binding technicians, huge screwdrivers in hand, stood planted in waist-deep snow pits, like garage mechanics, as racers pulled up for last-minute adjustments. Their bindings were cranked up to about 20, triple the setting of a good recreational skier's. I pulled a screwdriver from my pack and gave mine another twist.

"First forerunner."

My knees got weaker. I peeled down to my fancy orange-and-red racing suit (skin to win), its color and pattern happening to match those of Peter Mueller's and Pirmin Zurbriggen's. At least I *looked* like a threat. The day before, I had slowly run the course wearing my baggy warmups, the equivalent of deploying a small parachute. I'd looked like an ill-dressed geek but felt great. This, however, was the real thing. I'd even waxed my skis.

"Two minutes."

I sidestepped up to the starting platform, the 223s heavy on my feet. Officials hovered about, murmuring into their headsets. From this perch I could see many of the sunlit, snowcapped peaks of western Colorado. And from this perch, it was nearly two miles and 2,600 vertical feet down to the finish line and the valley floor.

"One minute."

I pulled into the starting gate, the electronic wand at shin level. My ski tips were poised at the lip of a steep chute that opened into a broad avenue. For more than a month, a full-time crew of forty workers had been preparing that avenue—grooming it, fencing it, wiring it. From here, it looked like a Christo sculpture—two parallel fences, one red, one blue, snaking down the ridgeline and rolling out of sight down Little Corkscrew . . . Zig-Zaugg . . . Aztec. . . . Somewhere down around the airplane turn, my fiancée, who for some reason thought this was all a good idea, was waiting.

"Thirty seconds."

I sucked in my breath. Behind the fences watched scores of officials and workers. At the crucial turns stood coaches from around the world. TV cameras poised on scaffolds every few hundred yards. Everything stared, nothing moved.

"Ten seconds."

The electronic timer started up.

"Beep."

"Beep."

"Beep."

"Beep."

"Boop."

I kicked hard out of the gate, strictly for appearance's sake.

The first part was easy. Crouching into a tuck, feeling good to be moving, I swept over the satiny snow, glistening in the early morning sun. Gravity sucked me happily along, the fences zipping by like telephone poles along a country road.

The gentle, rolling top half had three drops to it. The starting chute was the first drop. At the top of the second one, Little Corkscrew, a snowcat had heaped snow into a large bump. I saw it ahead, marked by the red panels of a gate, beside a dark knot of spectators.

I was moving faster now, the slope falling away, the wind beating about my ears. I stood up. There it was. I pulled up my feet hard to suck up the bump. . . .

"Zzzziinngqq." I launched out over Little Corkscrew, surprised at my height and distance. I hung airborne, feeling balanced, feeling good, feeling like the big boys. My skis hit with a slap.

Onto a large flat. Racers maintain maybe 60 miles per hour through here, folded low to the ground like high-speed beetles, thighs beginning to burn, skis perfectly flat. Mine suddenly began to weave—*The Big Swim*. I dug into my edges.

Under a TV camera and toward the third drop. Another bump, more spectators, more air. *Zzzziinngqq* . . . slap.

Down the third drop with its two small bumps—slap slap— and onto another long flat. I had plenty of time, as Doug Lewis had advised, to think about what was next. What was next, unfortunately, was Aztec and the lower mountain. From there, the next flat ground would be Garmisch Street, some 1,700 vertical feet below.

A difficult turn led into Aztec, a turn that young U.S. racers study over and over on video, watching how "Zubie" carves it without losing speed. Not me. I did not wish to go over the lip of Aztec at 40 or 50 miles per hour. I stood up and skidded my skis. The wind dropped to a dull flapping. I dumped so much speed that I almost pushed with my poles to get over the shady edge.

Then the earth disappeared. I dropped like dead weight down

a dim, icy cliff. First turn—my edges held. Second turn—I was doing OK. Third turn—almost no turn at all. I swept out of Aztec, the wind screaming in my ears, and hunkered down into my tuck, joyously dizzy with speed, feeling the roll of the entire mountain under my skis, giving myself to the terrain, to gravity.

I cut under the Ruthie's lift terminal, held my tuck toward a short drop called Spring Pitch, and . . .

"Whhhooooaaaa . . ."

Suddenly coming over Spring Pitch, I could see down into the bowl-shaped airplane turn. Despite the overnight work on the course, its surface was rippled and roughened from the previous day's training. At this speed the turn looked impossibly tight, the Berlin Wall looked very close, and my body no longer seemed mine but rather a heavy object moving at very high speed, answerable not to human will but to inalienable laws of momentum.

I plunged over Spring Pitch, caught air off the lip, got squashed by a compression at the bottom, and shot into the airplane turn, tightening up—bracing myself—when I should have been loose; leaning on my inside ski when I should have stood on the outside one. I skipped sideways over the ripples like a stone across a pond, my outside ski flapping up off the snow, thighs burning, centrifugal force sucking me toward the outside fences and spectators beyond. I almost lost it, but some deep instinct born for survival told me to hold on; no one wants to fall at that speed.

And then I was clear. I rolled out of the airplane turn, shot past the looming hulk of the Berlin Wall and onto a short piece of road. The worst was over . . . but what was that? Someone was snowplowing down the road, the equivalent of a deranged pedestrian strolling down the track at the Indy 500. I stood up, slowed

down, yelled "course!" The man finally pulled to one side and I
skied by, having lost considerable speed.

The course dropped off the road onto a steep pitch, and I
tucked to regain some speed. Suddenly I was going like hell
again. I braced myself. Then I was squashed earthward through a
deep compression, launched skyward over a roll, and slung far to
the outside of the course. (I *knew* there was a turn there.) I lost lots
of speed getting back on track. "You idiot," I said to myself. Lewis
again: "By the time you think about it, it's past you."

Three big turns to the bottom. No problem, unless you want
to win. For appearance sake I tried to hold a good tuck as I swept
through the finish turn, past the timing house, and under the
banner. I skidded to a stop in the finish area. If it were race day,
and I a real racer, fans would have been thronging the fences and
TV interviewers would have rushed in, microphones in hand,
asking what my thoughts were coming over the lip of Aztec. I'd
stand there, skis on shoulders, casually explaining, "Well, I *was* a
little worried about my wax being too slow. . . . "

But this was Thursday morning, and the finish area was deserted but for about twenty people, mostly officials. No cheers,
no throngs, no autographs. But wait. ABC's Bob Beattie!

"Hi," he said, and walked on by.

I thought I'd do better with my fiancée. I found her at the airplane turn, waiting for me to go down again. I informed her that
I'd probably taken my first and last run, that due to warm weather
and softening snow, the officials had just canceled some of the
forerunners. Was my fiancée happy that her loved one was finally
out of danger?

"I'm so disappointed," she said. "I wanted to see you do it
again."

On race day, the thronging crowds did arrive, maybe 10,000 strong. The sun shone intensely. By the 10:30 A.M. start time, the amphitheater-like airplane turn was heating up like a reflector oven. Thousands of tanned, cream-smeared faces lined its sides, displaying thousands of pairs of expensive sunglasses. Wearing tank tops, Hawaiian shirts, and bare chests, they sat on makeshift benches, small coolers conveniently alongside.

This was where the action was. The snow along the turn had become even rougher; to harden it up, course workers had sprayed it with a firehose and left it to freeze overnight. During the last training runs, racers came bouncing through in gorillalike positions, knuckles almost dragging, skis flipping and rattling over the ripples, a little like empty mail trucks speeding over a rash of potholes. Some of them blew apart; some simply skidded on their rear ends at about 60 mph, bounced up, and kept going; a lot of them, straining against the incredible centrifugal force, were pulled too far to the outside and missed the next gate. "Notice that the spectators all stand at the airplane turn," one racer told me. "For them it's like going to see *The Terminator*."

Through the training runs, Peter Mueller and Pirmin Zurbriggen clocked fairly close times. Mueller, meanwhile, had said he wouldn't wear his bib on the awards stand should he win again. (He said he promotes Porsche.) On Friday, in the last training run before the race, Zurbriggen beat him by a second. The headline in Saturday morning's *Aspen Daily News* gleefully proclaimed, "Mueller's String Threatened."

Like thousands of other bloodthirsty fans, I watched the race from the airplane turn, happy to be on the slow side of the fence. Michael Horn, the wisecracking, multilingual mayor of Kitzbühel, manned the PA system, sprinkling his commentary with a few bars of "La Marseillaise" in honor of a French racer, a few of "God Save the Queen" for a British one, and an account of how a Bavarian racer's wife had been left at home to milk her husband's forty cows.

Mueller would run in the tenth starting spot, Zurbriggen in the fifteenth. First out of the gate was Switzerland's Daniel Mahrer, who set a very tough pace with a 1:47:34. The two Austrians who followed were almost two seconds out. The fourth starter was Italy's enormous Michael Mair, who skis on 230-centimeter boards and weighs nearly that many pounds. (Pasta, he told me, tasted rather different when cooked at altitude.) His weight was an advantage on the course's flat upper reaches, and Mair clocked a nice run, trimming the Austrians' times by several tenths, good enough for fourth place.

Starting eighth, Doug Lewis swept through the airplane turn. The crowd roared for its native son, though Lewis probably couldn't hear anything over the scream of the wind; he would take ninth.

Then Mueller was on the course. Over the PA system Horn boomed that Mueller had just clocked the fastest intermediate time. Some guy down the fence from me was ringing a cowbell and yelling in a German accent, "Hup, hup, Pe-*tah* Muel*lah!*" Mueller came shooting out of Aztec looking big and strong like a Swiss racer should, bounced through the ripples, strained hard to the inside against the centrifugal force of the airplane turn, and, as if his earlier complaint about the course where prophecy, didn't make it. "He has missed! He has missed a gate!" announced the mayor of Kitzbühel. "Pe-tah Muel-lah will be disqualified."

By the time Zurbriggen came down, running fifteenth, ruts were forming in the sun-softened lower course. He chose an ex-

tremely tight line, skiing between the ruts and the gates—a tribute to his immense technical skill—and took the race in 1:47:29,
five one-hundredths of a second faster than his teammate
Mahrer. He also clinched the World Cup downhill title. Another
Swiss, Karl Alpiger, took third.

At the outdoor awards ceremony immediately after the race, a
swing band played "Boogie Woogie Bugle Boy," and a woman in
silver shoes and a leather miniskirt slipped about in the snow.
Officials introduced Robert Wagner and Jill St. John, who said:
"Isn't this just *fabulous?*" She wore a sparkling purple ski jacket; all
three Swiss politely wore their bibs.

By late Sunday afternoon the week was winding down. The
morning's super G had been won by Zurbriggen, and now, as
dusk fell, dark clouds began to spit snow. The lobby of the Continental was packed with racers, coaches, duffel bags, and a bab-
ble of foreign tongues. The skiers, civilianlike in blue jeans and
voguish street clothes, sprawled across armchairs watching golf
and tennis on two TVs. They were waiting for buses. Because of
the snow they'd have to drive, rather than fly, to Denver. The fun
was over; that gently oppressive Sunday-evening feel had descended with the dusk.

Of course, the life of the downhiller has its financial rewards,
at least if you win. And, sure, there's celebrity. During the week,
as I'd tromped around in my downhill suit, somebody from Aus-
tralia asked to pose for a photo with me, a bunch of little Aspen
urchins begged for souvenir buttons and pins, and a woman wondered how many servings I'd had for lunch. If this was the glamour and celebrity, I think you've got to love the work.

In the entrance hall of the Continental, the urchins had collared a Japanese racer, who signed a poster for them in big characters. Another Japanese translated: "Nippon Kamikaze."

I went upstairs for a while, and when I returned to the lobby, it was nearly empty. In the bar I saw pale faces, college kids from the East. It was dark outside by now, and a heavy, wet snow had begun to fall.

I went down to the basement to get my skis and it was deserted. The flourescent lights were on, but I didn't see a soul, just empty plywood cubicles with doors ajar, padlocks hanging. The skis, the technicians, the tape players, the rasp of files—there was nothing left. The circus had left town.

It didn't matter. I'd had enough sleepless nights. I'd indulged that adolescent fantasy. I found my big skis in the corner where I'd stashed them, slung them over my shoulder, and walked out through the dripping tunnel. The racers were traveling into the snowy night, bound for Calgary, for another downhill. I walked through Aspen's lamplit streets and the falling snow, headed for home and my fiancée.

The Dean of Flow

It was the third day of a spring snowstorm at Jackson Hole, and the wind was gusting to 40 miles per hour as I followed Doug Coombs off the tram and down the rocky summit to Corbet's Couloir. Six or seven skiers huddled there on the cornice and peered into its maw, squinting through the spindrift and summoning their nerve for the jump—a maneuver that's a little like stepping out a second-story window, except that you land not on the front lawn but on a 50-degree slope that drops another 500 vertical feet between two rock walls.

Coombs, lanky and wearing a black parka, sidestepped to a high point of the cornice—the peak of the house's roof—hopped off it about as casually as you or I might step from a curb, and then hung in the air for a lazy second or two, landing with a whump and swooping down the chute in fast, easy turns as if on a beginner's run.

It wasn't the jump, but the way he landed and carved his first few turns, that took the onlookers' breath away. You could almost hear the same thought running through everyone's brain: "Well, of course, I'll do it nice and easy. Just like that."

One by one, the rest of us dropped over the edge and—to put it in the parlance—splattered. A few augured into the snowpack below, others careened into one of the rock walls, still others somersaulted down the chute's throat. This was the third time in a week that I'd followed Coombs into Corbet's and the third time I'd crashed, duped by his understated execution.

A former downhill racer, and a geologist by training, the 34-year-old Coombs is arguably America's finest skier. A master of all conditions—especially very steep, very exposed terrain—Coombs has won the World Extreme Skiing Championships in Valdez, Alaska, two of the three years it's been held, and last winter he and buddy Jeff Zell took the Grand National Powder 8 Championships at Jackson Hole. Of course, he'd never agree to such lofty praise, arguing that there are plenty of world-class racers and unsung extreme skiers out there who are better than he is. So let's just say that Doug Coombs is a fabulous skier with a lot to teach the average intermediate. I'm a lifelong skier and a former racer myself, and I don't recall seeing anyone ski steep slopes with so much grace.

Raised in Vermont, Coombs saw his first serious slope—one with, as he puts it, "consequences"—at age 14, when his father, a cryogenics engineer, brought him along to New Hampshire's Tuckerman's Ravine. Coombs, too young to go to the top, watched awestruck from below as his elder brother skied the great cirque. "They were like gods," Coombs says. "They could ski it and I couldn't."

He ski raced during high school in New England and at Montana State University at Bozeman, then one of the nation's top teams. But instead of the slalom course Coombs's true love were the steep, rocky chutes that tumble through the cliffs above Bridger Bowl, the team's home area. Even on race days Coombs would hang out in the chutes carrying a pair of binoculars in order to watch the starting gate far below. "Just before our numbers came up we'd rip down the chute and show up at the start. The coaches would look at all the powder snow clinging to our clothes and say 'Where have *you* been?' But those chutes got the juices flowing."

The Bridger ski patrol dubbed Coombs and his ski buddies the Chuteski Brothers. It was on those same chutes above Bridger that Coombs, then possessing a wild head of hair and bushy beard, met Emily Gladstone, an MSU student and ski nut from New England. "Doug literally jumped off a cliff and landed at my feet," says Gladstone, who describes her first impression of him as "goofy."

After completing a geology degree, Coombs took up a classic ski bum's life working at carpentry or geology jobs in the summer and skiing all winter. It helped that he possessed what Gladstone

claims is an uncanny knack for finding money at the most oppor-
tune moments. For example, flat broke one summer in Hood
River, Oregon, where the famous board-sailors' wind always roars,
Coombs one afternoon spotted a stream of bills tumbling across
a parking lot and pasting themselves to the tires and driveshafts of
parked cars, from which he plucked them like ripe fruit.

Coombs and Gladstone harbor a certain nostalgia for those
simpler days before they gained their measure of fame. They
speak longingly of the "purists" of the sport—the unsung heroes
who climb and ski the chutes without the cameras rolling, without endorsements, without any reason for being there other than
the pure love of what they're doing. "We were purists once upon
a time," says Gladstone, who serves as Coombs's de facto advisor
and is a powerful extreme skier in her own right, having won the
Valdez women's division in 1992. "But now we get out in the pub-
lic world to make money so that we can ski."

It was a 1985 trip to Chamonix and a fateful encounter with
the great (and now late) French extreme skier Patrick Vallençant
that changed the way Coombs looked at skiing. He was sharp-
ening his edges one morning at the base of the lift at Brevant
when he saw a powerful-looking man walk past wearing a bright,
flowing scarf around his head and handling his skis as if they were
as light as toothpicks. Coombs and another Chuteski Brother,
Jim Conway, surreptitiously followed Vallençant up the gondola
and over a fence. Then they followed him as he rappelled into an
enormous, shadowy, ice-covered couloir that dropped more than
3,000 feet to the valley floor. "I got just about everything in that
chute—vertigo, sewing-machine leg," Coombs recalls. "At one
point I was hanging onto a rock ledge with one hand, slapping
my thigh with my other hand, and saying, 'Stop it! Stop it!'"

For that admission price, Coombs witnessed skiing at a "higher level" than he'd ever seen, as Vallençant worked the chute "like poetry." When Coombs stepped off the plane back in the States, he not only wore a scarf wrapped around his head, but was driven to learn to ski radical terrain, like his mentor, with consummate grace.

Understatement and quietness, even in harrowing places, are what now distinguish Coombs's style from that of other skiers. To see him ski is to see fluidity, as if he were a droplet of water trickling down a rough plaster wall: He squiggles along easily through the unobstructed patches, darts suddenly through tighter creases, and then resumes an easy trickle. "That's the most beautiful feeling—to flow down the mountain through intricate terrain," says Coombs. "That's the way I like to ski—to flow like water down the slope."

Of course, all skiers, no matter what their level, want to flow like water down the slope—or at least to finesse something close. So it was that I went to Jackson last winter with the hope of learning a few of Coombs's secrets. What I came away with was less a primer on how to ski than a different way to *look* at skiing.

One morning, I followed Coombs on a run that corkscrewed down a couloir, arced across a flat, soared off a ledge, skittered through a gully, leaped off a boulder, and swooped down a steep face that had alder bushes for slalom gates. After that I don't really know where Coombs went. He was still accelerating, but I had collapsed into an exhausted heap. The point of all this scribbling in the snow, I soon gathered as I watched the tails of Coombs's skis disappearing, was to practice the art of reading the mountain.

"Everyone has the same slope to start with," says Coombs. "It's all in how you interpret it. You create the run. You create the variety."

Coombs brings to his sport a geologist's talent for deciphering terrain and an ability to interpret and memorize unusual routes down unmarked faces. How many other skiers—extreme or otherwise—would describe their favorite runs as "skinny couloirs formed by vertical beds of eroded limestones and shales"? Key to Coombs's approach is seeing the mountain as a whole and employing so-called problem terrain creatively. Last spring at Valdez, for example, Coombs scanned the 2,500-foot snow-covered faces from below through binoculars to sketch out a route that linked the whole thing, instead of skiing it in short sections broken up by awkward traverses, as some competitors did. He mentally mapped a path leading to places other skiers didn't think to venture, searching out "obstacles"—a rock shaped like a rabbit's head, a swale in the snow—both to help him remember his route and to lend variety to his run. He calls this process route-finding.

Translating this approach for an intermediate skier at a resort, Coombs recommends what he calls "skiing across the grain" or "skiing the shadows." Because the most obvious route, usually down the center of the trail, gets compacted into ice or chiseled into bumps, it's best to gravitate toward the edges—the "shaded areas." Instead of avoiding obstacles like lift towers, trees, and boulders, Coombs suggests aiming toward them and trimming them as closely as you comfortably can. It's here that you'll find "islands" of powder, clumps of brush sticking up through the slope like impromptu slalom gates, and rolls and dips on what otherwise might be a flat, white-bread trail.

To add still more spice to your run, Coombs suggests that you choose several of these obstacles and "connect the dots," just as he does on Valdez's big faces. Duck underneath that lift tower, dive off that catwalk, shimmy through that patch of bumps, and don't stop to rest. Let the mountain suggest your style rather than forcing your style on it. On a good run you'll feel the shape of the mountain through the changing rhythms of your turns, the textures of the snow, the twists of its pitches. Says Coombs: "People looking up the hill should say, 'Look at that track. That guy had imagination.'"

"Think narrow," Coombs called out as I dropped ahead of him into a blind couloir called Alta One and a Half. Just around the first crook the rock walls suddenly forced me into the pencil-thin neck of the chute. I was uncertain where or how or even whether I could make the next turn in so tight a space, and I hesitated for a split second as I unweighted my skis. An instant later I heard the nauseating crunch of steel on granite as my tips plowed into the wall.

I hung there suspended, tips jammed into one wall and tails nearly touching the other, wondering what to do next. What I found particularly aggravating was that I knew exactly why it had happened. If I'd simply made more of the same crisp turns that had brought me to the bottleneck, I'd have sailed right through. But I had hesitated, choked, at the one place where I couldn't afford it.

There, wedged into the granite, I began to understand Coombs's mantra: "You have to flash the crux."

Coombs borrows from climbing terminology to define the crux as the most difficult part or parts of a run. He stresses two points to skiing it: Envision how you are going to ski it, and ski it hard.

My moment's hesitation in the crux of Alta One and a Half was a common mistake. "Half of the competitors at Valdez pause and look before they leap," says Coombs. "It makes sense, but you're supposed to have that terrain in your head. You have to be prepared to take some risks and accept what comes up in front of you. If you thought the chute was going to be 400 centimeters wide and suddenly it's 200, you have to be able to put your tails up on the rock to make the turn."

For Coombs, ripping the crux might entail squeezing through this 200-centimeter-wide couloir, or cranking a turn in front of a boulder in order to leap a rock band, or setting an edge on a near-vertical plate of ice. For an intermediate thrashing down his first black-diamond run, the crux becomes harder to identify. It might consist of simply an icy or bumpy patch, or the lip of a catwalk. Or it might comprise the entire route.

Whatever it is, be mentally prepared; clearing the crux is almost always a mental game. "In your head you have to do a quick flash of yourself skiing it," says Coombs. "Spot your mark, a rock or whatever, and then say, 'That's exactly where my skis are going to be, right next to that rock.' If you come at it saying, 'I don't know . . . I don't know . . . ,' you're going to have problems."

One way to become a bolder skier, then, is to pretend. Visualize yourself skiing that narrow right turn that's been giving you trouble: Your pole plants here, your skis turn there, you lean away from the slope and come down hard on your downhill ski to hold an edge on the ice. "The main thing is to flash it, rip it," he says. "You cannot pause."

Coombs insists so strongly on establishing the right tempo that if he's skiing a couloir and his first few turns feel awkward, he'll often stop, climb back up the chute, and start over again.

Tempo, that metronomic back-and-forth of making one turn after the next, probably grows out of our natural sense of rhythm, which in turn probably derives from the rhythm of our heartbeat, breathing, and pace while walking. In Coombs's language, you first set a tempo that starts slowly. (Says Coombs, "You can't let yourself go on the first turn.") If all goes well, the tempo then "blends" into a "flow," a trancelike state that accompanies moments when an athlete can do no wrong. "It's flow that sweeps you through the difficult crux moves," says Coombs. "You'll flash them, and then at the bottom you'll wonder how you did it."

I've experienced a few "flow" moments myself. You start skiing easily and slowly down a difficult slope, working your way into harder and quicker turns: back and forth, back and forth. It's a simple beat, and your confidence seems to build with each turn. Your body understands exactly what it's supposed to do. Your mind is wholly focused along a continuum that runs from your ski edges to the snow and on to the bumps and rolls ahead. Suddenly you know you can carve down that steep, icy patch. And then, simple as that, you do. That's how tempo leads to confidence, almost as if each turn were a swing of the hypnotist's watch accompanied by the words, "You can."

I saw a near-perfect example of tempo at work as I followed Coombs and his Powder 8 partner Jeff Zell down Rendezvous Bowl during a blinding storm. They were practicing for the world championships, where they'd be judged on the synchronicity of their turns and the perfection of their braided tracks in deep snow. The pair reminded me of a machine sputtering to life as they made their first awkward, jerky turns to their own rhythms, one behind the other. Then, they slowly found the same tempo, though their turns were still out of sync. Finally they meshed into perfect sync—left, right, left, right—while I fumbled through the heavy powder behind them. As they pulled away from me, they resembled not so much a machine as a swift, black bird beating its wings steadily against the whiteness.

A good tempo-improving exercise is to find a wide-open run and then create "stanzas" of turns, each stanza performed to a different tempo. First carve a set of four or five swooping turns—*shoooooo . . . shoooooo . . . shoooooo*—then pause a split second and shift the beat to short, tight turns—*choo . . . choo . . . choo*. Then pause again before opening up with some long *shoooooos*.

Closely related to tempo is pacing, a crucial element to consider when you're skiing long runs on big mountains. Strange as it may seem, Coombs spends a lot of time sandbagging on such runs—skiing less intensely on the easier parts—in order to save himself for the crux. Reading the mountain is integral to smart pacing. "You can be really wild and active for twenty turns, but there's no way you can do that for fifty," he says. "You have to know where the terrain will allow you to rest."

This is partly what gives Coombs's style its distinctive gracefulness—that quietness and economy of motion on even the most harrowing terrain. Jim Conway, who's an engineer by profession, describes Coombs's skiing this way: "Mistakes usually help define your style, but Doug just doesn't make any technical mistakes. In a word, I'd say he's efficient."

A few months after skiing with Coombs at Jackson, I climbed Oregon's Mount Hood to ski the summit chutes with him and Gladstone. As we picked our way along a knife-edge ridge that was defined by a precipitous drop a foot or two to the right of my skis, I desperately wanted off.

To my dismay, Coombs casually poked around up there, making a few jump turns amid small talk. Then he waltzed out onto an exposed spur, handing me his camera and asking me to take his photo atop a boulder perched over nothingness. "This is how you get used to the exposure and build your confidence," he explained as I attempted to hold him steady in the viewfinder while suppressing a bout of sewing-machine leg, "by playing around in places like this."

Every skier has his own definition of "steep," his own internal protractor that tells when it's time to panic. Steep might mean the headwall on an intermediate run or a rock-cluttered chute that even Coombs would call "pretty hairball." Either way, the steeps are where you're forced to put it all together.

According to Coombs, a good practice for the steeps is to ski among obstacles—trees, rocks, brush—on gentler slopes. Since a tree skier's option is to turn or eat bark, he learns to turn anywhere, anytime, an important skill to have in tight spots when the ground's atilt.

As you move your threshold for steepness out a few degrees, spend time hanging out in scary places, even if you have to walk your skis down. Ultimately, Coombs says, your first look down a steep run should tell you instinctively whether you can handle it. Once you do select a route, sidestep up the mountain a short distance and then make a few turns: the exertion will help calm any nervous trembling (yes, Coombs's legs shake, too). The worst thing you can do, he says, is to peer into the maw while you're waiting to go, "like all those people standing around at the top of Corbet's, psyching themselves out."

Just before taking the plunge, focus on these specifics: Know exactly where you'll make your first turn and visualize how you'll execute it. Keep your hands well forward and use some of what's known as "angulation"—leaning out over the hill—to keep your weight on your downhill ski. And stay low. Most intermediates stand too tall on scary terrain, but you have to get down and dirty, so to speak, as well as lean out. This lowers your center of gravity and puts you in a more athletic stance. Coombs also bears in mind the old racing (and boxing) adage, "float, then sting": Ski lightly between turns but come down hard on your edge-sets. "You'll be surprised at the places where you can hold an edge," he says. Finally, banish your doubts—you'll ruin your run by dwelling on what are euphemistically referred to as "negative thoughts."

I like to think of skiing the steeps as a spring cleaning of the mind. Since the run demands total concentration, there's no room for the clutter and static that usually crackles through one's head in the course of daily life. With each turn, as your legs compress and extend, you fall another notch down the mountain, waiting for the edges of your skis to catch and then release you again. Above you looms the enormous mass of the mountain; below you, gravity rules.

Standing on Mount Hood with Coombs and Gladstone, I looked down at a very steep snowfield dotted with jagged rock piles. As I tried to figure out whether my trajectory, if I fell, would take me into the rocks, Coombs took off skiing down the pitch.

"Don't the rocks bother him?" I asked Gladstone.

"That's the difference with Doug," she replied. "Where you and I see rocks, he sees patches of snow and the chance to turn."

The Road North: Arctic Travel

Driving to Greenland

JUNE 17TH, MISSOULA, MONTANA, MILE 0

It begins like any other summer vacation: Amy and I pay the last of our bills, take out the garbage, lock the apartment, and shake the doorknob twice. She eyes the contents of the VW van, which I've spent the afternoon cramming with everything from beach clothes to ice axes. "Are you sure this is everything?" she asks, a tinge of sarcasm in her voice. I pretend not to hear, and check my lists one last time; they certainly *look* complete. How can I know I'll later come up short one rod bearing for a 1974 Volkswagen engine? And a push handle for a four-passenger dogsled? And—if only I could've jammed it between the coolers and duffels—a landing strut for a two-engine Cessna?

This is one of those big undertakings that starts from a small notion. We didn't feel like spending another hot summer slouching around town, and so began to muse on the possibilities of clamping the cross-country skis into the roof-rack of our battered Audi, pointing her north on Highway 93, and going as far as we were able. When summer sends other American vacationers scrambling east to Europe, west to Asia, or south to Cancún, we would beat the crowds and aim for the great blank north. I was determined to prove that the same highways that meandered past our lawn sprinklers and petunia beds could whisk us—ok, maybe "whisk" is a little strong—all the way to tundra and icebergs. And, as long as we were in the neighborhood, I figured, why not shoot for Greenland?

For years, I'd wanted to visit it. From a plane seat I'd been taken by its fjords, granite spires, and the 14,000-foot-thick, 1,500-mile-long flood tide of the Inland Ice. I liked that it lay so far from the mainstream of modern life, that I'd never known anyone who'd been there, and that the entire population of this place nearly twice the size of Alaska could fit cozily inside an NFL stadium. In my mind, this white island—hanging above North America like a half-moon—came to represent a final, lonely bastion of Arctic life, enduring in its ways, a place where all the homogenized "Entertainment Tonight"-ified flotsam of modern Western culture is lost amid the frozen sea.

Of course, we couldn't drive the whole way. If the road gave out before we did, we figured to carry on by bush plane, motorized canoe, dogsled, whatever, until we reached the big ice cube itself. My father-in-law, Rags, volunteered to help drive the first leg of our sojourn. His qualifications were impeccable: a former White House reporter for the *Wall Street Journal*, World War II correspondent for *Time* magazine, and, important for this trip, a high prince of improvisational travel. He showed up on our doorstep with his debonair gray mustache and trademark bush jacket, plus his 17-year-old Volkswagen van, and promptly dissuaded us from taking the Audi. He told us he'd just had his engine rebuilt. Besides, he argued, you could sleep in a van. In fact, that's exactly where he'd slept a few days earlier when his starter motor died.

But now there is a new starter motor, and the van is ready to go. It sits on Front Street near a grove of cottonwoods whose leaves whisper in a soft June breeze, a sound for which I already feel a certain nostalgia. Rags takes his post beside the van. From the pocket of his bush jacket he pulls a battered Rollei camera that's served him well in Paris, Cairo, Manila, Bangkok. He hands it to a lady who is steering for the ice cream parlor down the street and asks her to take our photo.

We line up at the front bumper.

"Now smile." The woman brings the camera to her face. "Where're you headed?"

"Greenland," I reply.

"Greenland?" She clicks the shutter. "Now isn't that nice."

JUNE 17. THE CANADIAN BORDER, MILE 195.
All afternoon the van sails across the Montana ranchland like a prairie schooner, until forest closes in. We make the border at dusk.

Our fledgling career in exploration almost ends right here. I'm
at the wheel when the woman in blue runs through the usual
business on fruit, firearms, and felonies. I plead innocent, smile
amiably, and, wishing to avoid further suspicions, skip over the
issue of our destination. She's about to wave us through when
Rags's tousled silver head pops up behind me.

"Say, what if I'd brought my shotgun?" he asks.

For a moment, it looks like she might summon the Mounties
for a strip search. I swear to her that, despite the cross-country
skis, climbing ropes, Rags's canoe on the roof, and our assorted
other sporting goods, we didn't bring a shotgun. She listens skep-
tically and informs me that undeclared firearms can bring a
penalty of a $20,000 fine and four years in prison. Finally she re-
lents, confiscates two peaches from Amy, allows Rags to keep his
bear repellent spray, and admits us to the Great North.

Thus we begin our journey through the Canadian gloaming—
Canal Flats, Windermere, Radium Hot Springs. The sunset
lingers late, its orange transforming the Kootenay River into a
flaming snake.

Around 11 P.M. Rags takes the wheel, and Amy I climb under
the down bag in back. The van clanks slowly over the spine of
the Northern Rockies. Ear to the mattress, I listen for portentous
ticks or murmurs in the engine's whine. As I drift toward sleep I
imagine the sun tarrying just beyond the curve of the horizon
and envision the van haltingly working its way up the bulge of
the planet like a beetle up a basketball.

Certain questions occur to me: Does AAA tow above the Arctic Circle? How far north do you have to go before people stop
speaking English? How strong is the market for used German au-

tomobile parts in the Northwest Territories? At what temperature does gasoline freeze?

JUNE 18. BANFF NATIONAL PARK, CANADA. MILE 325.

At 7 A.M. Amy and I jolt awake, shaken by the rumble of a passing trailer truck. We're in the parking lot of a Petro-Canada station, 10,000-foot mountains on every side. Rags, who can sleep
anywhere, lies in the van's narrow aisle, where he wedged himself for a catnap three hours ago. The station was closed when he
pulled in, and by his reckoning the next one is about a hundred
miles up the road.

The attendant arrives, and we trail him to the station's door
like lost ducklings.

"Every night when we close up, the lot's empty," he tells us,
"and every morning when we come to work it's full of people
sleeping in their cars."

We fill the tank, buy tea and doughnuts, and hustle back onto
the road. The van's air-cooled engine whirs along like a Swiss
watch. We belly out of the Rockies and roller-coaster over long
hills cloaked in spruce and fir—the taiga that girds the earth
around the 60th Parallel. In seven hours of driving we encounter
three towns:

Muskeg River. Very tiny.

Grande Cache. This resembles an Eisenhower-era subdivision
air-dropped into a forest clear-cut. Schoolgirls in pigtails cavort in
pink pedal-pushers. "Well, I know the town's two years younger
than I am," says the young woman working the gas station's cash
register, "so that would make it twenty-one. I think it was built for
the coal mine, but now we've got a pulp mill and a jail."

Grande Prairie. Sitting on a vast bald patch in the spruce in-
terspersed with grain elevators, this town could well be in Iowa.
At 8:30 P.M. at Zeller's Department Store in the Prairie Mall,
women with red, orange, and black perms maneuver shopping
carts between bins of white sneakers. In their carts I see a life pre-
server, Rollerblades, wicker picnic-plate holders, a set of folding
chaise lounges, an electric fan, and venetian blinds. Out in the
parking lot I see a seagull circling a lamppost and wonder just
where the hell we are.

JUNE 20. MACKENZIE HWY. ALBERTA, CANADA. MILE 1,000.

At 6 A.M. Amy and I wake to a slackening in the van's sway as Rags
pulls to the shoulder. He points to our position on the road atlas.
I notice his empty coffee cups stacked in the dashboard holder.
The sun hangs low over the spruces, which seem to be shorter
than yesterday's spruces, and the highway ahead slashes straight
through them like a swath cut through a wheatfield. We unlatch
the doors—time to change drivers. Rags still wears his bush
jacket. No cars up here. There's an eerie silence but for the soft
strains of "Great Baroque Adagios" from the tape player and the
whine of mosquitos from the bush.

Rags crawls under the sleeping bag.

"It never really got dark last night," he reports, and falls asleep.

Amy accelerates northward in search of breakfast. A few miles
up the road at Indian Cabins we come upon a café and abandon
Rags to his slumber in the van. Arlene, the proprietor, slaps Amy's
French toast onto the griddle, whacks at my breakfast steak with
a cleaver, and tells us that the café is a reconstructed Hudson's
Bay Company trading post, trailered in from somewhere east.

The place smells of pine smoke, which Arlene says is from the cured moosehides she buys from the nearby Slavey Indians.

While she cooks, Arlene tells us how, twenty-odd years ago, she came north from the Saskatchewan prairies to build roads for a Canadian government that wanted to lay its claim to the territory. "They're still trying to fix 'em right," she says. "One place the road's melted into the permafrost, and each year the crews try to pave over the same dip. Of course, each year it melts out a little more, so now they've got asphalt twelve feet deep."

"It must be very peaceful living up here," Amy says between bites.

"There isn't much pressure for conversation," Arlene replies laconically. "It's different up here. We still help each other."

"Because of the cold?"

"Right. In winter, if you see someone standing beside the road you pick them up even if they're repulsive or drunk."

JUNE 21. YELLOWKNIFE, N.W.T., CANADA.
MILE 1,411.

Road's end. We've crossed into the Northwest Territories at the 60th Parallel, forded the Mackenzie River on a ferry, and skirted Great Slave Lake. The van has clunked from narrow asphalt onto narrower gravel until we've reached Yellowknife, which Rags pronounces the ugliest town he's ever seen. Like us, he had envisioned a few cabins tucked by a lake with birchbark canoes pulled up on the beach, but Yellowknife possesses the unfortunate honor of being both the territorial capital and the hub for the region's gold-mining industry. Its drab six-story office buildings poke from the taiga like some Bulgarian office park, but its prices are Parisian. As I hoist various bags from the van toward

Rags's $125-a-night hotel room, a man weaves along the sidewalk toward me, stoops down to help me lift my pack, and topples over at my feet.

After checking in, Rags chauffeurs Amy and me to the airport. Today, the longest day of the year, is balmy, shirtsleeve weather, appropriate for a happy parting. We unstrap the duffel bag, which is stuffed like a sausage with skis, crampons, mittens, climbing ropes, parkas, and bits of deer and bear hide that an old Arctic hand has recommended we carry as gifts for the natives up North, and load it into the plane.

In the terminal, father and daughter hug good-bye. Rags plans to canoe for a few days near Yellowknife, then drive the van 4,000 miles to New York City. He'll leave it for Amy and me at one of his old haunts in Greenwich Village. To get there, she and I will have to travel the Great Circle Route.

Our forty-passenger turboprop plane drones northward. I press my face to the window. Rags and his van disappear, and I look out at the landscape. A lumpy shield of rock, dusted with greenery, potholed with thousands of lakes, and rent by domes of granite, extends to the horizon. I can't make out a road, a house, a power line, a single mark of human presence, a fact that I find oddly comforting. We soon cross the Arctic Circle. A few rows back, an Inuit man cradles a water-filled plastic bag that flashes with tiny, darting tropical fish.

"A lot of people up here have them," he says. "They're easy to keep, and kids love 'em."

We climb over a cloud bank, and when we get our next views of the terrain an hour later, the granite shield has splintered into rubbly pans, low islands, dark peninsulas. Great white plates of sea ice grind against the shore. Up here the polar cold has scoured the green from the rock so that the earth appears bald and naked. I understand the tropical fish.

All evening the plane hopscotches northeast across the Canadian Arctic, swooping down at Inuit villages like a bus pulling over to a curb. Finally, it drops us for the night at Pelly Bay. We descend the aircraft's rear steps, and my hands stiffen in the 38-degree breeze. The sky is a heavy gray. Waiting for the passengers in front of the terminal is a rainbow phalanx of Inuits in ski parkas trimmed in lime, orange, and hot pink. They gently greet their relatives and friends, swing their legs over ATVs or climb into pickups, and bounce off across the tundra. There's not a dogsled in evidence. We stand shivering in the wind off the sea ice and marveling at the strangeness of this place. Today, Amy reminds me, is the first day of summer.

JUNE 22-24. PELLY BAY TO BAFFIN ISLAND. MILES 2,345–3,745.

The turboprop drones onward across the Arctic: to Igloolik, Hall Beach, and Iqaluit, on the southern end of Baffin Island, where we meet Horst and Lieselotte, a German couple who've hired a five-passenger plane to fly them north. Horst is an international lawyer, Lieselotte a watercolor artist who's completing a book of Canadian landscapes and wants to see the Arctic. They've kindly agreed to give Amy and me the two extra seats on the two-engine Cessna Skymaster. The plane is owned by Jacques, a young Air Baffin pilot who has abandoned a stockbroker's career in Montreal to fly the North.

When Horst gets a glimpse of the minuscule airplane he's hired, he hands his big camera to a bystander and motions the rest of us to gather near the craft.

"Vee must take von last picture vhile vee are still ah-life!"

It takes us a good ten minutes to stuff ourselves into the plane. Imagine a compact car, fit its roof with wings, and cram it full of skis, ropes, easels, suitcases, backpacks, sketchbooks, and five full-size adults. For three days we hold cramped positions as Jacques leapfrogs us among the villages of mountainous Baffin Island. We eat bags of chocolate-chip cookies and buzz over ice caps, stony peaks, creamy white clouds. I'm reminded of old black-and-white movies and their cottony portrayals of heaven; I almost expect to hear strains of angel choruses mingling with the throaty buzz of the engines as we motor through the sky like carpoolers heading for church in some airborne Honda Civic.

Jacques feathers the plane over the immaculate whiteness of an ice cap, a white that's as thick and bottomless as the blackest night.

"You go back to the South," he shouts over the plane's noise, "and it will never be the same again."

JUNE 25-26. BAFFIN ISLAND TO QAANAAQ, GREENLAND. MILES 3,745–4,265.

Jacques lifts our plane off the northern end of Baffin Island, jumps Parry Channel, and brings us late in the afternoon to the southern coast of Ellesmere Island at Grise Fjord, the northernmost village in Canada. We're now less than a thousand miles from the Pole. From the air the village is nothing but a few dark specks at the foot of a huge glacier-topped headland. Lieselotte counts them.

"Ten houses!"

The plan is this: Lieselotte and Horst will hop the next plane back, while Amy and I will hire Jacques and his plane to fly us the 225 miles across Smith Sound to the Eskimo village of Qaanaaq, Greenland. The weather, however, keeps us pinned down overnight. Suddenly, on the morning of the 26th, Jacques announces that it's time to go.

There is no terminal, no control tower, no one to see us off. The plane sits at the foot of the glacier-capped headland like a moth beside the Superdome. Jacques stands on a paint bucket and swabs the windshield with a roll of paper towels. We climb in, Jacques revs the engines, and we quickly rise to 9,000 feet in a blue sky streaked with high clouds. I look back at the tiny cluster of houses as the plane swings out over the sea ice. Through the radio headphones I hear only a cold, dead static; I wonder how long our little party could hold out on an ice floe.

A pattern like window frost etches the ice below; then the ice fractures, and I see tiny waves on the dark sea. The plane whirs over clouds for what seems a long time, its shadow forming a tiny cross that skips through the cumulus below. Jacques is attired in his usual white button-down shirt, a relic from his stockbroker days. It is with some gratitude that I finally hear over the earphones that we've been picked up by the radar of Greenland's Thule Airbase. They report we're nearing Qaanaaq, and Jacques pushes the plane into a steep descent and tips it through a hole in the clouds. We're suddenly winging 600 feet over a dark, glassy sea studded with icebergs.

"Ooof!" Jacques exclaims, and ducks both his head and the Cessna as a flock of lesser auks zips past in quick black streaks. "Ooof! Too many focking birds."

Amy and I call out bird alerts while Jacques veers the plane accordingly. We enter a giant, ice-covered fjord in which two flat-topped islands hunker like aircraft carriers. Two miniature caravans wend across the ice shelf—actual dogsleds.

Jacques locates the airstrip, bulldozed into the tundra on a bench above town. Someone has lit a red smoke-flare for us, to indicate the wind direction. Jacques dodges the village's radio mast and satellite dish, and glides the plane down into an approach. But the instant before the wheels touch, he guns the throttle and pulls back on the controls.

"Too much speed."

On the third circle he goes for it. The wheels bump once. I feel a wave of relief—Greenland at last.

The plane suddenly lurches dangerously to the left. Jacques snaps upright in his seat and wrestles with the controls as the Cessna fishtails down the runway like a car on an icy highway. There is a tremendous grinding of rock against metal. The plane wallows into a sideways skid, drags its tail and left wingtip through the dirt, and finally jerks to a stop, its nose tilted skyward.

The billows of dust blow away on a breeze. There hasn't been time to be scared. Jacques jumps from the plane, followed by Amy. Sitting in the backseat, I vaguely wonder if the plane might explode. I dig my way from under the bags and crawl out the door into a numbing wind off the frozen fjord.

It's odd what one notices at such moments. Two hundred yards from the airstrip sits a little cemetery planted with white crosses. This adds to a certain survivor's euphoria that now infects our little party. Amy snaps photos of the crippled plane while Jacques hops about marveling at the events and running his hands over the damaged left landing strut, which lies on the soft, sandy runway. It then happens that I glance toward the village. A careering, twitching caravan of four-wheel drives, pickups, and fire trucks is bucking and lurching across the rocky tundra. It appears to be making for us.

JUNE 27. QAANAAQ, GREENLAND. MILE 4,266.

They don't ask for passports. There is no customs check. The fact that Qaanaaq, like the rest of Greenland, is in a foreign country—part of Denmark—doesn't strike us until we begin to notice the village's quiet mixing of Inuit and Continental culture. At the village's co-op, ten feet from the Danish pastry counter, stands a freezer case stuffed with bricks of frozen whalemeat. People wear tony pink corduroys with sealskin boots, and newly married Inuit couples wrestle baby strollers over the rocky tundra. The local soccer field—surely the world's northernmost sports arena—is plowed off on the sea ice. Qaanaaq's dirt streets are neatly kept, its colorful, steep-roofed houses evoking a Nordic fishing village, yet in the yards stand dogsleds, needle-thin kayaks of hand-stitched canvas, and game-butchering platforms caked with blood.

Qaanaaq, which lies a mere 800 miles from the Pole, is the main village of the Thule Eskimos, the northernmost people in the world. Their dozen or so hunting villages have been kept isolated from Greenland's warmer south, as well as from the rest of humanity, by several hundred miles of glaciers and sea ice. A Lutheran minister, Hans Egede, began the Danish colonization of southern Greenland in 1721, but it was nearly another century before the Europeans realized that anyone resided in the northlands. The feeling was reciprocal: Until 1818, when British explorer John Ross's ship appeared off Cape York, the Thule Eskimos believed they were the last people left in the world.

After Ross, Scottish and American whaling ships ventured close to these frozen shores, followed by a small tide of polar explorers. Denmark's Knud Rasmussen and Americans Frederick Cook and Robert Peary learned much about Arctic survival by wintering with the Thule Eskimos. Peary also took an Eskimo wife, and today many of Qaanaaq's residents proudly bear his last name, including the chief of police, Robert Peary, who can be seen patrolling the village with a pair of handcuffs and a cellular telephone.

The welcome to outsiders wore thin in the early fifties when the United States placed its Thule Airbase at Ummannaq, square in the middle of the best hunting grounds. The Eskimos moved their main village 80 miles north to Qaanaaq, but thanks to some far-thinking social policies they've managed to hold on to many of their old ways. Instead of issuing subsidy checks as the Canadian government does to support its Inuit populations, the Danish government has legislated low prices throughout Greenland, meaning that Qaanaaq's hunters can afford fuel, ammunition, and other necessities. Further, Qaanaaq controls alcohol by a strict point system, under which adults can purchase no more than ten beers a week. And, perhaps most significant, the local Hunters Council has banned the snowmobile in favor of the dogsled.

That evening, while Jacques goes to work repairing his plane, Amy and I check into Qaanaaq's little guest house. We meet two windburned Danish walrus researchers who tell us that out at the "ice edge"—20 miles or so out to sea—we'd find Thule hunters who stalk narwhals with kayak and harpoon. They give us the name of a hunter who can take us there.

"That is where you should go," they say, "if you wish to see something truly different."

JUNE 29. MIDDLE OF WHALE SOUND. MILE 4,267.
The day is glorious, at first. Amy and I smear our faces with sun-
screen, our young interpreter, Vittus "Vito" Qujaukitsoq, dons his
wraparound shades, and we three recline shoulder to shoulder on
the wide band of caribou skin on our hired dogsled. The dogs fan
out at a trot, attached to a central harness in the Greenlandic
style, and their paws flip-flop merrily toward us. The frozen fjord
extends beneath the blue sky, icebergs thrust from it like broken
teeth five stories high, and the great mass of the Inland Ice peeps
above the mountains like a rising moon.

"Harruuk! Harruuk! HAA-CO!" the driver shouts. The whip
cracks, and the dogs veer left around a green puddle of meltwater.

Whip in hand, pipe in mouth, Thomas Kivioq, 57, is a small,
wiry man with a lively sense of humor. A hunter by trade, he has
agreed, for a price, to sled us to the narwhal hunters at the ice
edge. Vito, 19, is the son of a hunter but is headed toward a different way of life. Cheerful and broad-shouldered, he's fresh out
of a five-year stint of schooling in Copenhagen and will enroll at
interpreter's school down in Nuuk, Greenland's capital. He's also
the founder of the world's northernmost tae kwon do club and,
by his own admission, is not much of a hunter. "It's my secret that
I've never taken a seal before," Vito confides to Amy and me.

Our ride can't quite be described as gentle. Every minute or
two the dogs plunge into a puddle of meltwater, and the low-
prowed sled crashes down after them, slides across the slushy
bottom, and thunks up the other side, our heads jolting chiro-
practically from side to side. Through hundreds of puddles we
mush onward, hour after hour. Though it's brilliantly sunny, the
wind isn't your typical June breeze. Amy and I have on our full
winter gear and still suffer ice-cream headaches from the cold

blast. Thomas and Vito, for their part, sit calmly on the sled and scan the ice for seals, picking out black spots that I need binoculars to see.

"Aiy, aiy, aiy," Thomas says gently, a command that halts the team.

A few hundred yards off, a seal lies sunning itself on the ice near its breathing hole. Thomas pulls his rifle from the sled and hands it to Vito.

Vito awkwardly begins to assemble the white cloth screen that the Eskimo hunters push ahead of them on a tiny sled as a blind.

"You do that like a *qallunaaq*," Thomas quips, taking the screen and assembling it.

Vito laughs—the word means "big eyebrows and belly," a term Thule Eskimos traditionally reserve for southerners. Then he begins to stalk. Soon Vito is crawling over the ice behind the blind, as he's seen his father do, the gunbarrel mounted through a hole. We hear the sharp crack of the rifle. The oblong black shape shudders, then remains on the ice as if asleep.

Amy and I leap onto the sled, and the dogs charge toward the dead seal.

"Maybe we have a future hunter here," says Thomas.

We lash the animal, a big ring seal, to the front of the sled and set off. Dark clouds now boil to the north. Vito begins to tell us about his laser-disk video system. The wind sharpens. Thomas aims the sled toward the fuzzy outline of Qeqertarsuaq Island. Vito begins to list his favorite movies. The sled bucks down into a puddle, slides over the slushy bottom. *"Total Recall, 48 Hours, The Terminator . . ."* The sled jolts up the far bank, jiggling the blubber of Vito's seal. "Patrick Swayze, Eddie Murphy, Arnold Schwarzenegger . . ."

JUNE 30. QEQERTARSUAQ ISLAND. MILE 4,280.
We're pinned down by a snowstorm on the island's southern
shore, where we have pitched camp on a bouldery strip of beach.
Nothing's to be done but eat and sleep and listen to the tent flapping in the north wind. Thomas periodically climbs the stony
slope behind camp and scans the ice with his binoculars. The ice
conditions are worsening, he reports, and water is pooling
deeper. This is the *avanneq*, the north wind that can blow the entire floe out to sea. Still, Thomas says, we have a chance to reach
the narwhal hunters. And so we wait.

We watched Thomas feed the dogs the night we arrived, lay-
ing the seal out on the cobbled bench and expertly peeling back
the skin as if it were a tube sock. He offered Amy and me a piece
of liver, which we gingerly shared, although Vito refused it, having lugged a duffel full of canned goods with names like Weiner
Gryde and Spaghetti Napoli.

We while away the hours drinking mugs of tea in Thomas and
Vito's tent, where Thomas's Primus stove hisses away, heating the
tent like a sauna. I ask Thomas how far he's traveled by dogsled,
and he tells me of the four times he's crossed over to Canada to
hunt polar bear and the time he escorted an Italian explorer to
the Pole. Give a choice, Thomas said, he prefers a dogsled to a
snowmobile. Machines scare away the game, and dogs don't
break down far from home. They also know to stop at the edge
of an *aineq*—a crack that splits the ice and upwells with black
water. Besides, the snowmobile ban, along with the prohibition
on the use of motorboats for hunting narwhals, keeps up game
populations. I ask him about hunting, and he jokes that now that
he is older he prefers caribou, because they are easier to shoot.
When I ask him about seal hunting, Thomas grows quiet and

Vito steps in and explains that Greenpeace's late-seventies protests against killing baby harp seals has ruined the market for sealskins generally. Qaanaaq hunters usually take only ringed seals, which remain abundant in the Arctic and don't congregate in large groups to give birth like the harp seal, which had been an easy target for the clubs of white commercial hunters 1,500 miles south in Newfoundland, the focus of Greenpeace's protest. But now times are tough. As Vito and Thomas talk, I begin to appreciate the irony of their people's situation. The first wave of white men asked the Eskimo for help in killing the whales, the second wave paid handsomely for the sealskins, and now the third wave tells the Eskimo that they shouldn't kill anything at all. The Eskimos I spoke with didn't find this ironic; they simply wondered why anyone would want to alter a way of life they've been striving to preserve.

JULY 1. STILL AT QEQERTARSUAQ ISLAND.

It's still snowing. This is our third day in our tents, and the ice has grown worse. We've decided to abandon the search for the narwhal hunters and return to Qaanaaq at the first opportunity. The snowfall relents late in the afternoon, and we push off. We ride for hours without stopping except when the dogs' traces get tangled or when Thomas has to maneuver a chunk of ice into position as a bridge across an ever-widening *aineq*.

The sled plunges through the puddles, and the dogs' paws leave a trail of red blood spots over the rough white ice. Vito, struggling to shoulder the sled over an *aineq*, accidentally rips off the sled handle. The weather deteriorates—first sleet, then snow, then wind. A freezing fog blows in, dropping a curtain of white

around us that disorients me completely. Thomas sits in front
with his whip, holding the dogs to a steady course.

"How does he know where he's going?" I ask Vito.

Vito asks Thomas in Inuktutut.

He says he doesn't know how he knows," Vito reports. "He just
knows."

For nine hours we jolt along—clunk, scrape, clunk. Our heads
are lolling, our clothes are soaking, and no one says much, as if
we've buried ourselves in our thoughts to keep warm. My toes are
numb, my hands freezing, my torso sopping, and I'm trying to as-
tral-project myself to some warmer, cheerier place.

Vito turns to me. I notice the droplets of snowmelt that have
beaded on the tips of his spiky haircut.

"Maybe now you can understand why I don't want to be a
hunter."

We drive on in silence, but for Thomas's commands to the
dogs. Icebergs loom out of the mist. The wind batters our faces.

Amy turns to me.

"I've been thinking," she says, brushing the flecks of snow from
her wind-reddened cheeks. "Maybe next summer we could go to
a place with outdoor cafés."

AUGUST 15. MISSOULA, MONTANA. MILE 9,301.
In the end, we stayed at Qaanaaq for three weeks, not because
Jacques didn't repair the landing strut—but simply because we
liked it. One day, however, we gathered our things, said our
good-byes, and climbed aboard the twice-weekly helicopter
down to Thule Airbase. Two hours later we stepped into the
base's club with its candlelight, wine list, and steaks with bear-

naise sauce. From Thule we'boarded a U.S. military cargo
flight—it was like a flying grain silo—and made our way south to
Nuuk, where we hopped a commercial flight over to Iqaluit, then
Ottawa, finally arriving in a jam-packed subway car that slowly
trundled into Manhattan on a Sunday evening during a heat
wave. We balanced in the aisle with our backpacks stuffed with
mittens and parkas, while around us pressed a carful of T-shirted
beachgoers, coolers, grills, sun hats, boom boxes, bicycles, and a
woman who drank from a quart bottle of beer and alternately
hugged and slapped her small boy.

Rags's van was waiting for us in Greenwich Village, and Amy
and I drove it west. It would ultimately fail us, burning out its
crankshaft bearings on a steep mountain pass near town. We
called Rags, and he had us put it in the shop for an overhaul. He
said he wanted it to go another 40,000 miles before its retire-
ment.

We made it back, eventually, and on our first night home
someone broke into the van and stole our camping gear, discard-
ing what they didn't want into the Clark Fork River. After our
long loop to the top of the world, that's where the trip really
ended—with the odd bits of gear and books about the Arctic
washing up on the river's rocky shore.

Land of Fire and Ice

The change in climate was abrupt. Just a few hours earlier, I'd been squirming in the steamy August heat, battling legions of disgruntled drivers on the Illinois Tri-State Tollway. But up here, near the Arctic Circle, everything was orderly and quiet and green, washed by a refreshing wind. Up here, it was heavy sweater weather.

The little airport sat at the end of a long, deep-blue fjord, flanked by grassy mountains capped with snow. Out in the fjord, a big white passenger ship rocked gently at anchor, its stack emblazoned with a hammer and sickle. Farther down the shore was the town of Akureyri, its clean architectural silhouette inviting closer inspection. Cool and serene, Akureyri seemed the place to pause and renew frayed nerves.

But there was no time for resting. A Russian-built rent-a-car waited in the parking lot, ready to be loaded with a mound of duffel bags, backpacks, climbing ropes, ice axes, and skis. There were three of us—myself, photographer Raymond Gehman, and our 20-year-old Icelandic mountain guide, Olafur "Óli" Baldursson. We were on a journey to Iceland's simmering center.

This Ohio-sized island is one of the most intensely volcanic regions in the world. Imagine two huge chunks of the Earth's crust—called plates—floating on the magma of the planet's interior. On one of these plates rests the North American continent; on the other sits Europe. Between them runs a long crack in the Atlantic floor where the two plates are pulling apart, millimeter by millimeter. As they move, magma wells up between them, adding to their mass.

The Earth grows here. The fissure is called the Mid-Atlantic Ridge, and Iceland—half in Europe, half in North America—sits astride it. Riddled with volcanoes and punctuated with glaciers, this is the land of fire and ice.

Iceland has been called one big national park. It hasn't a tree worthy of the term, but it does offer steam jets, hot springs, boiling mud pots, and the spouting spring known as Geysir that gave that natural phenomenon its name. It has fjords, mountains, and countless waterfalls, in addition to bizarre natural events like the *jökulhlaup*, massive flash floods occurring when volcanic heat melts glacial ice. One finds deserts, ice caves, towering grassy headlands, and black sand beaches. And in the island's barren, un-inhabited interior, the landscapes are so vast and so desolate that they seem illusory, the work of a Hollywood special-effects artist rendering the surface of a strange and distant planet.

And then there are the volcanoes. Since 1500, Iceland's volca-noes have accounted for an estimated one-third of the Earth's output of lava. I asked an Icelander if any were erupting at the moment. "Not today," he replied, "but maybe tomorrow." A few weeks later, one of them blew.

A volcano on Iceland's west coast served as the starting point for Jules Verne's *Journey to the Center of the Earth*. Our journey was overland, our destination a place near the geographic center of volcanic activity, high in the glacier-tipped mountains of Ice-land's interior. We were seeking the place where fire and ice meet.

To envision our route, forget about trees and paved roads. Then imagine Iceland from far above. It looks like a rough and barren rock, patched with ice and rimmed with green.

Our journey was a trip back through time, taking us from the modern cities of Iceland's lush coast, through its quaint and pas-toral coastal valleys, to the island's volcano-dotted, rock-and-ice interior. There we were at the source, where the Earth is new.

Icelandic discos open around 11 P.M. and start filling about mid-night. Suddenly they're jammed with boisterous youths dressed in chic European fashions or in full punk regalia—shades, leather, miniskirts, leopard-skin pants. As the evening progresses, the scene could be compared to a remake of *Animal House* directed by Federico Fellini.

They shout at each other, they hug each other, they fall on each other, they dance madly to music from both sides of the Atlantic. You meet characters like the skinny academic who's standing in the men's room, drunkenly singing "Yankee Doodle"; the middle-aged artist who immediately asks if you know of Jack Kerouac; the woman who drums in a rock bank; the political types espousing at length on international politics. It's a rowdy but nonviolent crowd, and at 3 A.M. when the discos close, hundreds of merrymakers gather on the sidewalks out front, deciding which party is next. It's said that the island is home to the world's largest nightclub.

This was not the place I'd envisioned. As a rocky North Atlantic island, Iceland, one expects, would be a bastion of salty fisherman and rustic shepherds. But this vision doesn't allow for cities like Akureyri or Reykjavík, the nation's cosmopolitan capital of 85,000. There, I was the rustic—especially in those discos.

Urban Iceland—what there is of it—has the look and feel of the future. The cities are all concrete and prosperity. Akureyri and Reykjavík are built around quaint, European-style waterfront districts, but their outskirts, notably Reykjavík's, are a maze of newly poured cement. There are concrete high-rises, concrete two-story homes, and concrete ranch houses, heated with hot water pumped directly from the ground.

They are not large cities, but they are large enough by North Atlantic standards. "In Akureyri," says a big, blond youth, a resident of that city, "it takes maybe one hour to walk from one side of town to the other; in Reykjavík, it takes maybe 24 hours."

As for prosperity, statistics show that Icelanders enjoy one of the world's highest standards of living. Almost no one lives in poverty, and unemployment is less than 1 percent. Car and home ownership is common; longevity and infant survival rates are impressively high. Despite disco madness and a reputation for alcoholism, Icelanders drink less than other Scandinavians. They don't drink frequently, but when they do, they drink hard.

Iceland also boasts a strong social welfare system, a tradition of egalitarianism (the nation's president is a woman), a large cooperative movement, and a high rate of illegitimacy (no social stigma attached). Icelanders maintain a deep love for literature (universal literacy was achieved in 1800), no military (although the United States has a base near Reykjavík), the world's oldest surviving democratic institution (the Althing, or Parliament, founded in A.D. 930), and very little crime (one armed robbery in recent history). Even in Reykjavík, you almost never hear a siren. It's the kind of place where you might meet a cabinet minister in the grocery checkout line, and where the busy lobby of a downtown bank is outfitted with children's tables laden with building blocks.

Orderly and prosperous, it's a very modern society with very old roots. Although Iceland used to be a nation of farmers, much of its current wealth is derived from its coastal waters. Icelanders enjoyed a brief era of prosperity after the island's settlement 1,000 years ago, but then sank into centuries of poverty and isolation. During the nineteenth century, however, Icelanders began to acquire decked boats to take advantage of their exceptionally rich fishing grounds. Fishing is now the mainstay of the Icelandic economy.

One finds fish on the tables and fish on the coins. Fish factories border harbors full of fishing boats. Fish racks bear thousands of rock-hard dried fish that click softly in the winds that sweep through coastal villages. "The life in Iceland," said Halldór Laxness, the nation's Nobel-winning novelist, "is fish."

The pavement ended at Akureyri's outskirts; the clock started to wind back.

Óli, a premed student and member of Iceland's elite mountain-rescue group, was at the wheel of the big Ford Bronco we obtained by trading in the Russian rent-a-car, which had a suspension that tilted oddly to the right. From the fishing town of Akureyri on Iceland's north coast, we headed south across Iceland's green rim to its steaming rock-and-ice interior. That, at any rate, was the plan. As we bounced along a grassy mountainside above Akureyri and its fjord, I asked Óli if this switchback-ridden gravel track was considered a good road by Icelandic standards.

"Yes, very good," he replied earnestly, swerving to avoid some sheep.

We crested the ridge, putting Akureyri behind us, and looked down into the next valley. The clock clicked back about 300 years.

Gone were the concrete high-rises and fish factories of the coastal cities and towns. The valley, and those beyond it, looked like a remote sector of the Scottish Highlands, decorated with Scandinavian architecture. Sheep populated the grassy hillsides, and little white villages nestled on the valley floors, their red-roofed steeples jutting toward a broken blue sky. Crystal-clear streams tumbled toward the sea.

All afternoon we twisted through verdant valleys and little white hamlets. It is here—away from the coastal cities—that one feels Iceland's thousand-year past.

It was largely an agricultural past, and a harsh one. During their centuries of isolation, Icelanders had to be self-sufficient, yet this was not easy in a climate where most grain will not grow and where 80 percent of the land area is classified as glaciers, lava fields, and "other wastelands." Only 1 percent of the land is arable; here farmers grow hay, turnips, and potatoes. Hay, Iceland's main crop, feeds the island's dairy cows, sheep, and the sturdy, sure-footed Icelandic horses that are used to bring sheep down from high-mountain pastures.

Agriculture, in the form of family farms, is still very much a part of Iceland. At the farm of 54-year-old Einar Kjartansson we saw Icelandic self-sufficiency in action. A startlingly beautiful place, it fronts a black sand beach and is backed by grassy ridges topped with glacial ice. This particular pocket of the coast is known as Reynishuerfi. There are no discos in Reynishuerfi; it consists of eight farms and a little church, and is named after a man called Reynirbjoern, who settled here about A.D. 900.

Einar lost his sheep to disease a few years ago, but he and his sons showed us the milking barn, with its thirty cows and milking machinery; the small outboard boat from which the family, in three frantic days last year, caught two tons of fish using hook and line; and the puffin net, a bit like a butterfly net with a long handle, used by hunters who hide on cliff tops, waiting for passing birds.

When the day turned windy and rainy, we sought refuge in the large, modern, one-story farmhouse. As the rain lashed the kitchen windows, we sat down to a hearty meal of turnips, boiled potatoes, and cod drenched in a mild-flavored melted sheep's fat called *tolg*. Dessert was one of Iceland's national dishes, *skyr*, which tasted like an especially rich yogurt and was topped with milk, sugar, and shredded lettuce. "Except for this little bowl of sugar," said Einar, "everything we are eating comes from this farm."

After lunch, two of Einar's sons and a young cousin visiting from Reykjavík drove us in an ancient Land Rover along the black, storm-tossed beach. There, Gretar Einarsson demonstrated the traditional method of catching grounded seabirds, a technique that involves a stunning kick to the head and quick bite to the soft part of the bird's skull. The bird then will be salted and eaten.

Early in the morning of our second day of driving we came to a junction in the main dirt road. A primitive jeep trail split off, marked by a sign that pointed across a vast, barren volcanic plain: "Kverkfjöll—105 km."

Civilization ends here; we had crossed Iceland's green, inhabited circumference. Beyond was the interior desert, and beyond that, far off on the horizon, was Kverkfjöll, a snow-crowned range that seethes with volcanic heat. Kverkfjöll, the Throat Mountains, was our destination.

We bounced onto the jeep trail, and the clock whirred backward.

The track looked like the trail of a runaway bulldozer. We plowed through soft sands, jolted over lava rocks, and splashed through glacial streams that coursed down from the distant mountains. We fixed a flat, lost the trail amid a labyrinth of lava formations, and ate smoked herring beside a raging glacial river.

I hadn't seen a tree since I'd left the far side of Chicago. The terrain alternatively resembled a giant gravel pit, the wide-open salt deserts of Utah and Nevada, and a black and twisted lunar landscape. Not far from here, American astronauts had trained for the moon landing.

The clock spun back millennia with each mile. It seemed we had entered a time before life began—before cars, houses, animals, bushes, or birds. We saw nothing but the occasional patch of lichen and a few blades of grass, reminders of the first simple organisms struggling for a toehold on a landmass newly thrust up from the sea. The region appears to need a few more eons to smooth out the rough, raw edges that make it look like a massive construction site.

Saint Brendan apparently thought so, too. One of Iceland's earliest visitors, he was frightened away by a flaming mountain, perhaps the first recorded eruption of an Icelandic volcano. Many others have erupted since then; along with related cataclysms and natural disasters, these eruptions have shaped Iceland's history in somewhat the same manner that the histories of other European nations have been shaped by war.

In the early sixth century, so the legend goes, Brendan and a few other Irish monks were blown off course to a point near Iceland's shore. The monks heard noises like thunder, saw a mountain "shooting up flames into the sky," and were confronted by a "savage man" who charged down the shore throwing hot slag at their little boat.

"Soldiers of Christ," Brendan exhorted the monks manning the oars, "be strong in faith unfeigned and in the armor of the Spirit, for we are now on the confines of Hell."

Brendan's flaming mountain is believed to be the volcano Hekla, which in later centuries became known as the gateway to hell. Its presence, however, did not deter other Irish monks, who established a short-lived settlement on Iceland by the late eighth century, nor the Vikings, who first visited in the ninth century and who, after a particularly unpleasant winter, gave the island its name. Iceland's first permanent settlers arrived in 874, led by the Norwegian Ingólfur Arnarson. In the next sixty years, a period known as "the Settlement," other immigrants, many of them Norwegians, came to Iceland and claimed all the island's arable land.

What followed was a brief golden age. Despite some years of famine and hardship, the Icelanders exhibited a bold spirit. They founded the Althing, a governing body for a nation of free men, which met annually near Reykjavík in the south. Meanwhile, Icelandic literature flowered with the creation of poetry and the famed "sagas," those detailed, realistic, and often-violent heroic stories that eventually were set down on parchment. This adventurous spirit also led to far-flung geographical exploration. The Icelanders colonized Greenland; from there; Leif Eriksson set sail for the distant coast known as Vinland—North America.

The good years came to an end about 1300. The nation's political stability had been upset by internal feuding, the adoption of Christianity, and Norwegian meddling. In 1262 the Althing agreed to pay allegiance to the Norwegian throne. The ensuing centuries have been called the "Dark Years." Icelanders were battered by eruptions, natural disasters, and plagues, and burdened with taxes and trade restrictions imposed by the Church, Norway, and finally Denmark, which incorporated Iceland into its kingdom in 1380.

The island seemed to turn against its inhabitants. Agricultural production faltered as the climate entered a centuries-long cold cycle, exacerbated by soil erosion caused by overgrazing. Then came a series of enormously destructive eruptions, including that of Laki in the 1700s, when ash and gases ruined the grasslands,

killing over half the island's sheep and cattle, and causing famine
and disease that claimed nearly 10,000 lives. After this disaster,
Denmark proposed that the Icelanders simply abandon their island and move to the Continent.

The Icelanders hung on, however. In the nineteenth century,
their economic well-being began to improve with the development of commercial fishing, and their political autonomy grew.
In 1944, Iceland won complete independence from Denmark,
and in the postwar years its economy boomed.

The destructive eruptions, however, continued. In 1973, lava
rolled through the fishing town of Vestmannaeyjar on Heimaey
Island, destroying over 100 homes but stopping short of the invaluable fishing harbor, which was saved when millions of tons of
cold seawater were pumped onto the advancing wall of molten
rock.

The 60-mile-long jeep trail ended at the foot of Kverkfjöll, and
we spent the night in a hikers' hut at the end of the road.

The mountains mark the northern edge of a glacier known as
Vatnajökull which, at about 80 miles across, is larger than all the
glaciers in the Alps combined. A long tongue of the glacier tum-
bles like a river down to the valley floor. Far above the hut, just
behind the peaks, we could see the heavy white form that is Vatnajökull's main mass; among the peaks we saw faint puffs of
steam. Our destination was high on those mountains, about a
day's hike away.

In the morning, we parked the car on top of a rocky moraine,
shouldered our heavy packs and started up the glacier's tongue.
My spirits, bruised as they were after that long, brain-rattling
drive across the desert, rose with each step.

I'd envisioned a mass of hard-packed snow; this glacier, how-ever, was ice—solid, massive ice, wet and translucent like the block in a beer cooler on a hot summer day. The entire mass was moving downhill, ponderously and imperceptibly, its surface busy with rushing water. Crystalline rivulets of glacier-melt zigzagged through smooth-bottomed channels, their sounds mingling in a sort of Icelandic symphony—the crashing of the large streams, the hollow gurgling of small streams, the drip, drip, drip of tiny rivulets. We filled our bottles and drank deeply; the water was the best we'd ever tasted.

The ice steepened, and we began to slip and slide. With cram-pons lashed to our boots, we climbed higher, to the accompani-ment of the rhythmic crunching of sharp metal points biting into the hard, wet ice.

At times we had to skirt crevasses, big cracks in the glacier that descend far into the blue-green ice, eventually vanishing into the blackness and untold depths. At one point, our path was blocked, and Óli stepped across the two- or three-foot-wide crevasse. I paused. A movie ran through my head: the hero leaps from the roof of one 20-story building to the roof of the next, while the pursuing villain steps a little short.

I survived this small step, but started calling the bigger crevasses "keepers," a reference to stories about animals that have fallen in and been locked in the ice for centuries, eventually being dis-charged at the glacier's leading edge. I peered into the crevasses and designated them according to depth—"a hundred-year keeper," "a five-hundred-year keeper. . . ."

All day we climbed. The higher we went, the colder it got and the harder the wind blew. The hats and gloves came out, and we unstrapped our skis from our packs. Up here, the glacier was covered with snow.

Finally, we mounted a broad, wind-swept ridge that was covered with a dome of slushy ice. At the crest of the mountain range, the view opened up. Ahead of us to the south was the flat, white expanse of Vatnajökull's main mass; to the northwest was the eeriest, most desolate landscape I'd ever seen.

In the far distance were snowy peaks topped by ominous clouds, while at their base was a large plain engulfed by a sandstorm kicked up by screaming winds. On the near edge, the plain was bordered by a huge, flat tongue of Vatnajökoll, its surface studded with big black rocks and patterned with miles-long zebra stripes of dark earth. Which planet was this, I wondered.

Óli pointed out the sights, explaining that an ancient road runs across the vast plain, leading from Iceland's north coast to the south. After hearing that the name of the road translates roughly as "Exhausted Horse Road," I imagined a lone traveler on horseback pushing through the sandstorm toward the distant Althing, determined to cast his vote.

In the late afternoon, we reached our home on the glacier—a small wooden hut, unheated but solidly built, maintained by the Icelandic Geological Society. It sat atop a steep little hill that protruded from the ice. The knoll, for whatever reason, is called Bensíntunnutindur—"Gasoline Barrell Hill." Just below it is a pothole in the ice holding a small glacial lake, and beyond that is Vatnajökull, stretching to the horizon like the polar ice cap.

Gathering around the small wooden table, we relaxed in the warmth and candlelight as evening fell. We cooked our freeze-dried stews on portable stoves, laughing about the package of "smoked baby horsemeat" that I had inadvertently picked up in

an Icelandic grocery. The wind outside made the shutters vibrate
and beat the triple-layered door against the walls, sounding like
a snare-drum section manned by wildly happy Icelandic gods.
Perhaps they were glad to have us within their easy reach. In Iceland, Óli told us, natural phenomena are given human names; the
wind, he says, is "Kari."

We were now very far from anywhere. To reach the nearest
house, we would have had to walk a day to the car and then drive
five hours across the desert. But we were very near our destination. In the morning, we would search for fire and ice.

The morning was sunny and windy; the climb was brief. From
the top of a steep ridge we looked down into a small valley surrounded by mountains on the flank of an old volcanic crater filled
with ice.

Jules Verne could just as well have started here. The valley's
barren hillsides were colored a rich ocher, contrasting with a
deep blue sky; on its floor was a small lake sprinkled with little
icebergs and backed by the white wall of Vatnajökull. The valley
was alive. From its hillsides, from its floor and from vents in the
glacier shot jets of steam that streamed away on a strong southwest wind. The valley basked in the Earth's interior heat.

We paused on the ridgetop. I felt as if a secret was about to be
revealed, and never revealed again. Then we leapt down the hillside, running and jumping in the springy soil, descending to the
valley floor.

We peered into hot springs, the steam boiling up warm and
moist against our wind-chilled faces; we walked along a hissing,
steaming hillside, backing away when the ground seemed hollow; we skirted the glacier, the steam rising gently along its edge.

I touched my finger to a small hot spring, jerking it back before I was scalded.

We were near the Mid-Atlantic Ridge. Heat originates in the planet's hot center and wells up through that big crack where the Earth grows and the continents are pulling apart.

We heard a soft rumbling. It came from a hole about 20 feet wide, veiled in clouds of steam. We walked closer, stepping carefully.

A gust of wind parted the steam to reveal a witch's caldron churning with a thick, gray-green liquid. Suddenly its surface jumped with a tremendous boil, pushing up a two-foot-high bubble that burst in a cloud of steam and a splatter of mud. "There's something down there," I said, "something big."

The mud pot erupted again. Around us the lake ruffled in the cool wind, and the glacier moved a tiny bit closer. On the hillside the steam jets hissed and whispered like voices from the planet's core. "The Earth is alive," they murmured.

The Earth is forming here. The dirt and rock were born in volcanic eruption; now they are shaped by Vatnajökull's icy, slow-moving mass as it plows into the rocky hillsides, pushing through the soft dirt and feeding the waters of the little lake that someday, perhaps, will support aquatic life.

The clock had spun to zero; we'd arrived, in a sense, at the Creation.

Perhaps we saw too much in the hot-spring valley, displeasing the Icelandic gods. That afternoon, we were pummeled by a fierce windstorm as we hiked and skied the glacier. At one point, Raymond broke through the surface, plunging waist-deep into a snow-covered crevasse. He dangled briefly, his fall toward the depths having been arrested by the skis he carried and the rope he was tied to, and quickly scrambled out. The wind was so strong it staggered us sideways, and the airborne ice particles stung our faces, but Óli, somehow, led us safely across a maze of crevasses to the shelter of the hut.

In the morning, we headed out. The winds had slackened, as if in apology for yesterday's tempest. As we walked past the little lake just below the hut, a chunk of ice the size of a small car split from the glacier and crashed heavily into the water. "It's Vatna-jökull," I said, "bidding us goodbye." The air became warmer and calmer as we descended, and by the time we reached the stony plain at the glacier's foot, a deep evening quiet hung over the landscape, broken only by the rush of a distant glacial river. It was a bare-rock-and-dripping-water quiet, a middle-of-the-desert quiet. This was a place, said Óli, for what the Icelanders call "Hlusta á thögnina"—listening to the silence.

Finally, the clock hands began creeping forward. We started the long drive back to civilization, following the jolting track through the desert toward the twentieth century.

We didn't get far. About a mile into the drive, as we were climbing a steep knoll, the road suddenly jogged to the right. We went straight.

The car bounced over big lava rocks and came to a stop, leaning precariously over a steep but short embankment. We were surrounded by half-buried rocks. We couldn't move forward, we couldn't move back, and the car seemed dangerously close to tipping. The nearest house was a five-hour drive away; we could have waited for days for someone to show up. Someone softly began to sing: "It's a long way/To Akureyri. . . ."

We set to work, tying down the car with climbing ropes, constructing a ramp of lava rocks to take us back up to the road. Underneath the car big lava rocks protruded from the earth. The only way out was to break them apart.

We climbed under, and, using smaller rocks as primitive hammers, started pounding away. We tried to free this hunk of high-tech metal from the primordial desert, using Stone Age tools to clear a path toward civilization, toward the fish factories and discos of the distant green coast.

The clock had jammed. Thwack . . . thwack . . . thwack, the sound of stone on stone drifted across the silent, empty plain.

A Kinde
of Strange Fishe

At 10 P.M. the sun hung so high in the northern sky that it looked like midafternoon. The polar sea was mirror-smooth. Chunks of ice whispered lazily on the incoming tide and brushed against the ice floe to which we'd anchored our boats, about 15 miles out in Hvalsund—Whale Sound—a great notch cut into the mountainous coast of northwest Greenland. That's when I first heard it—a series of hollow, rubbery exhalations that surrounded us as if we'd stepped inside an air mattress that someone was inflating with enormous puffs.

Mamarut Kristiansen, an Inuit hunter, pulled on white gloves and drew his matching hood over his black, tousled hair so that only his weather-burned face showed. He wore soft sealskin boots, and now he stepped delicately into the cockpit of his off-white kayak. He wriggled his legs into the narrow, sharp hull, adjusted the harpoon lashed to the deck and, like a seal that flippers its way over the ice, palmed himself to the edge and slid into the sea. The other hunter, Sigdluk Miunge, stood beside me wearing a pair of polar-bear leggings. He gestured at my stop-sign-red parka; I let it drop to the ice. Immobile as statues, we watched Mamarut's kayak slice through the sea, aiming toward the rubbery breathing.

A few weeks later and several thousand miles to the south, I recalled that suspended moment of white and ice and waiting. My wife, Amy, and I were then at Port Townsend, a quaint harborfront on Puget Sound, attending a kayak event of an entirely different spirit, not to mention dress—the West Coast Sea Kayak Symposium. Polar-bear pants were not in evidence here. Instead, participants walked barefoot through the warm sand in purple shells, lime-green shorts, and fluorescent baseball caps embroidered with brand names. Scores of kayaks in hot pink, bright yellow, and sky blue lay strewn along the beach, while out on the water a pod of forty or fifty paddlers skittered about like waterbugs on a frog pond. I couldn't imagine what Mamarut or Sigdluk would make of this busy, benign, rainbow-hued gathering, but to me it underscored the point that the kayak—this ancient hunting tool—has traveled 8,000 miles and 9,000 years and recently has exploded into a Technicolor sport: sea kayaking.

Tracing that passage, Amy and I came to appreciate the kayak as one of the most ingenious crafts ever designed. It's a boat whose lines one early Russian missionary described as "so perfect . . . that even a mathematician could add very little," and whose centuries-old hull shapes might teach something to the designers of modern ships. Today's recreationists likewise have discovered that, among paddle-powered boats, the kayak has no equal for its graceful combination of lightness, portability, seaworthiness, and speed. And, too, that in its resemblance to a "kinde of strange fishe"—in the words of one of explorer Martin Frobisher's chroniclers—it is also unrivaled as a craft from which to view sea life. In short, the kayak is a boat that has been astonishing us southerners ever since Frobisher's party arrived off Baffin Island in the 1570s and learned the hard way that a single Inuit in a kayak could easily outdistance twenty British seamen in a longboat who yanked at their oars in hot pursuit.

It's impossible to pin down the exact time and place of the kayak's invention. One theory places it in the vicinity of Alaska's Aleutian Islands about 9,000 years ago. To settle the islands, the Aleuts would have needed the kayak's seaworthiness and extreme speed, because the Aleutian chain sits among some of the North Pacific's strongest currents and roughest waters, which remain ice-free year-round. The mummified remains of ancient Aleuts found in burial caves testify to their reliance on paddle power in the enormous size of their arm bones, compared to which the arm bones of Russian explorers look like "pipe stems," says University of Connecticut anthropologist William Laughlin.

From the Aleutian area the kayak probably spread north to the Bering Strait and east across the Arctic as far as Greenland, according to Laughlin. Vikings encountered Inuit in kayaks during their explorations of North America and Greenland about A.D. 1000.

The Europeans who sailed north seven centuries later searching for trade routes and furs were struck with "amazement beyond expression" at these tiny, skinny boats in which the pilot sealed his torso to the deck with an apron of whale guts so that man and boat became a single, waterproof unit that paddled *through* the waves as well as over them. The boat was so remarkably strong but light that the kayaker could ride the surf to shore, hop out, and walk down the beach with his kayak under one arm, while the envious Europeans foundered offshore in their heavy wooden boats, unable to land. Kayakers in some parts of the Arctic could flip themselves over if an unusually large wave approached, then swiftly right themselves with a sweep of the paddle and a flick of the hips after it had harmlessly washed past their overturned hull. "They are so confident in them," one trading captain reported, "and so vers'd in the guiding of them, that they shew a thousand tricks in them . . . diving and rouling themselves in the Sea three or four times together; so that they may be taken for perfect *Amphibia*. . . . "

Today, the kayak survives as a hunting vehicle only in the most remote pockets of the Arctic, such as areas of northern Canada and the Thule district of northwest Greenland. Unlike most residents of the North American Arctic, who rely on snowmobiles and all-terrain vehicles for getting around, the local governing council in northwest Greenland has banned the snowmobile in favor of the dogsled—in part because the machine's racket frightens away game—and requires that hunters use the kayak when they stalk narwhals. These small whales, whose males sport a unicorn-like horn, grow to about 16 feet.

When I first tried Sigdluk's kayak, I couldn't squeeze my size-11 feet beneath the low foredeck or jam my thighs or rear through the hole of the tiny, round cockpit. This was slightly embarrassing. I removed my rubber boots at the hunter's suggestion and hopped about in my stocking feet over the ice, but, even as Sigdluk and Mamarut helped stuff me down into the cockpit, I didn't fit. "Each kayak is different, and each man builds his kayak to fit himself," Sigdluk explained as I struggled to extract myself. "It can't be too big, and it can't be too small."

We'd met the hunters only a few days before, on a sunny afternoon in early July, when Amy and I had found Mamarut Kristiansen standing in his hunting whites, eating a hamburger topped with shredded red cabbage at the counter of the Polar Grill. This resembled just another hot dog stand in, say, Ohio, providing you ignored the view out the front door of the five-story icebergs embedded in the half-frozen sound. The Polar Grill sits on a rocky street in the middle of Qaanaaq, a town of about one hundred houses that looks a bit like a Scandinavian fishing village dropped on a gravelly headland; there are a few bulk-oil tanks, radio masts, dozens of kayaks, and hundreds of howling sled dogs.

That morning at four—clocks don't count here in the endless light of summer—Mamarut had dogsledded across the ice of Whale Sound into Qaanaaq with a load of *mattak*, the hornlike skin of the narwhal that is a Greenlandic delicacy. With a handshake, Mamarut, a stocky, energetic, fun-loving man in his early 30s and son of a famous former walrus hunter named Masauna, agreed to take us out with him. Thus it was, a few days later, that we left his two-room house on Qeqertarssuaq (Herbert Island) and, with the kayaks lashed to the gunwales of his and Sigdluk's small motorboats, we headed across Whale Sound. We beached the boats, with a slow crunch of ice against fiberglass, on a great floe. "And now we can wait for hours and hours and hours," remarked our interpreter, Vito, once more.

Mamarut sharpened his harpoon; his girlfriend, Tukummeq Peary—a great-granddaughter of Robert Peary—chewed a piece of sealskin to soften it for a pair of boots; and I poked my head into the cockpit of Sigdluk's kayak. I studied the way he'd lashed the ribs to the keel with tightly wrapped sealskin line, because, he explained, nails can break or work loose in rough seas. Now 60, Sigdluk said he had learned how to make kayaks from the old men when he was young. His had a spare, simple, elegant design with knifelike bow and stern, and low, slightly sweeping deck, that reminded me of the thinnest sliver of a new moon. Its canvas skin was stretched drum-taut over the stringers, and the carefully stitched seam formed a gentle S along the deck. He'd painted it light gray to mimic the skin tone of a narwhal calf.

In years past he'd used sealskin instead of canvas, but it was a lot of work to hunt five animals and scrape the skins, and very difficult to sew the seam inside and out. And then you had to replace the whole works periodically. Old kayak coverings were thrown to the sled dogs to eat, which explains why hunters store their kayaks up on racks out of the dogs' reach.

Sigdluk had used a measuring stick to build his boat. In some parts of the Arctic, hunters used proportional formulas; the diameter of a Hooper Bay kayak, for example, is the distance from the armpit to the fingers' first joints. In this way each kayak exactly fits the man who built it. Likewise, the kayaks of each region evolved over the centuries to meet the demands of local conditions and prey. The Caribou Inuit of Hudson Bay preferred a round-bottomed kayak for its extreme speed and maneuverability in chasing fast-swimming caribou, even though it was tippier. The Bering Sea kayaks incorporated a sloping, roof-shaped deck to shed the heavy seas that broke over them in those rough waters. The kayaks of the Aleuts—which some say represented the state of the art—featured a peculiar "wide-tailed" stern that, experts believe, caught trailing seas to propel the boat forward or reduced drag at high speeds, as well as a bifid bow, which resembled a fish swimming along with its mouth open, its narrow lower jaw slicing through the water.

The exact function of this bifid bow remains something of a mystery and has caught the attention of nautical circles. Kayak historian and designer George Dyson believes that the upper part of the bifid bow provided dynamic lift to help the kayak rise smoothly to meet oncoming waves, while the lower jaw reduced the waves made by the kayak itself. Under certain conditions, explains Dyson, the underwater projection created a wave trough that countered some of the drag induced by the waves made at the bow. This is the same principle on which today's shipbuilders give freighters a bulbous underwater bow projection. For the Aleuts, the advantages would have been a quieter approach in stalking prey, as well as improved paddling efficiency and speed.

The Aleut kayak, which evolved over thousands of years, seems to have incorporated elements of hydrodynamic design that remain unclear to the still-imprecise field of fluid dynamics. Unlike our rigid-hulled ships, the elastic membrane of the Aleut kayak was supported by an ingenious skeleton that included a jointed three-piece keel. Both the skeleton and the keel were equipped with as many as sixty bone or ivory bearings that, according to anthropology graduate student Joe Lubischer, allowed the boat to flex easily and noiselessly over the waves. Other Aleut refinements included waterproof padding jackets sewn from sea-mammal intestines; hulls stitched from the scarred and battle-toughened skins of the seal's or sea lion's neck; and, to shield their faces from rain and sun glare, hats of bentwood that looked like long-billed baseball caps and were topped with a mane of sea-lion whiskers that lent the paddlers the aspect of seagoing royalty.

In Qaanaaq, by contrast, kayak and dress were designed with great emphasis on stealth and invisibility during the narwhal hunt. "If you build it too wide here," said Minik Daorana, one of Qaanaaq's best builders, running his finger along the sharp bow of one of his boats, "it will make small waves, which make noise and frighten the narwhal." Qaanaaq's hunters stroke with long, narrow paddles that have slightly flattened ends to cut wind resistance, and also to minimize light reflection and drip, either of which can frighten prey. That first day on the ice floe, I watched Mamarut trim the stray wood fibers from the end of his paddle blade with a knife, so the paddle would come cleanly out of the water without dripping.

By then I'd managed to yank my lower legs from Sigdluk's kayak. Mamarut suggested I try his. Boots off, I was able to slither down into the slightly roomier cockpit. Mamarut grabbed the stern and slid me off the ice edge into the sea. Bobbing beside the floe, I held tightly to it with the paddle blade, reluctant to push off. I'd done a lot of canoeing and a fair bit of whitewater kayaking in my life, but this was altogether different. For one thing, I wore no lifejacket. In fact, I hadn't even *seen* a lifejacket in the Arctic; up here, they figure that the water's so cold, you'll die in a few minutes even if you're wearing one.

Also, I wasn't sure I could extract myself from the kayak if I tipped, I'd jammed myself in so tightly. I had a quick, dark vision of hanging upside down in the polar sea, legs trapped under the hull, as a pair of ringed seals frolicked past my burbling head. I'd read that champion Greenlandic kayakers know twenty-seven different techniques to roll themselves upright. I knew how to do one of these "Eskimo rolls" in a river kayak, but I wasn't at all confident about executing the intricate maneuver in this one. Mamarut, to my surprise, didn't know how to roll it either. "So what would you do if you tipped over?" I asked him. "Drown," he replied.

Gingerly—very gingerly—I pushed myself away from the floe. I rocked my hips a bit to get a feel for the kayak. It was quite stable. I made a few cautious strokes. It glided easily toward the evening sun, which poured a quivering, golden film over the glassy sea. Gaining confidence, I paddled harder; the kayak responded by streaking along like a hollow-bodied arrow, seemingly straighter and swifter than the modern kayaks I knew. I remembered what Mamarut had said: "The most difficult thing is to paddle silently and so the sunlight doesn't reflect from your blades." Spray spun off my paddle blades in crashing waterfalls, and I was probably reflecting more light than a mirrored ball at a high school prom, but the ride sent a thrill through me as I cut between ice floes against the stunning backdrop of glacier-capped mountains.

For dinner that first evening on the ice floe Sigdluk fired up his campstove and boiled the party a pot of *inaluaq*—bearded-seal intestines. The snow crunched under our boots as we squatted around the pot and burned our fingers as we split open lengths of gut with our pocketknives. We stuffed them with wedges of seal blubber and gobbled them like hot dogs slathered with the works—fuel to stoke the body's furnace against the polar climate. The sun dipped slightly toward the northern horizon at midnight, chilling the air and congealing the sea with lacy fingers of ice. Amy and I huddled deeper in our sleeping bags in the bow of Mamarut's motorboat, while the hunters crowded into Sigdluk's boat for a raucous, all-night card game. It looked like Uno except that when they had one card left, instead of saying "Uno" they shouted "Olsen!" into the sun-charged midnight air.

For three days we remained camped on the ice like that, periodically moving from one floe to the next, up and down the channels, scanning and listening for the narwhals. We passed the time wrestling on the ice, sleeping, chatting on the walkie-talkie. The kayaks lay at readiness with harpoons tucked under deck lashings, and lines coiled on the foredeck as meticulously as a crocheted potholder. A fouled harpoon line, I learned, could kill the hunter. The system works like this: one end of the line is tied to the harpoon's detachable steel or ivory point, the other to an inflated sealskin that rests on the rear deck like a stuffed pig (plastic floats, they told me, are too brightly colored). Sneaking up behind a swimming narwhal, the hunter seizes the harpoon off the deck and spins it overhead.

As it strikes the narwhal, the shaft drops away and leaves its point embedded in the flesh. The alarmed narwhal dives, and the line sings out from the coil on the foredeck. At this crucial juncture the hunter adeptly knocks the sealskin float into the water. The float drags behind the fleeing narwhal to slow its escape and mark its place. When the tired animal surfaces, the hunter approaches for the kill.

The system is precise, difficult, and emblematic of the exacting and finely focused nature of subsistence in so raw and cold a land, where it's not possible simply to sow a few seeds and grow a patch of wheat. I'd heard one account of a hunter whose paddle snared in the line so that the fleeing narwhal jerked boat and occupant down to the depths, like Ahab, until the hunter popped up some moments later and some yards away—minus one finger.

At times during those three days the game of Olsen in Sigdluk's boat was suddenly halted. The hunters paused in midhand with cards help up like fans, heads cocked. Off in the distance I'd hear that hollow, rubbery breathing; the hunters threw down their cards and jumped for their kayaks. I watched Mamarut, dressed in white and paddling his off-white kayak, as he slalomed between the broken floes. The rubbery breathing grew closer— the sound of inner tubes and hookah pipes—but when I looked again for Mamarut, he'd vanished. Now, where he'd been, I saw just another chunk of broken ice floating on the tide, but this one, I knew, carried a razor-sharp harpoon.

It's particularly ironic that the same features that have made the kayak such a lethal hunting tool—its stealth, low profile, unobtrusiveness—have brought it great popularity with whale watchers and other wildlife lovers. "There's something nice about the fact that you're going roughly the same speed as animals in the water," said kayak guide Michael Singer, one evening a few weeks later as we sat around a driftwood fire on a rocky beach in Washington's San Juan Islands. "Rather than whizzing by, when you see a seal from a kayak, you're kind of an equal."

Earlier that day, accompanied by Singer and fellow guide Jerry

Lanz, Amy and I paddled a tandem sea kayak across a choppy channel from Orcas to Cypress Island, with our tent and sleeping bags stowed—dry—in hatches in the beamy plastic hull. Lanz identified Bonaparte's gulls, Dall porpoises, and harbor seals that surfaced near our boats and, heads cocked to the side, eyed us curiously.

No hard statistics exist to document sea kayaking's explosive growth in the past decade, although one marker is that more than 200 sea kayak models have appeared on the market only since the late 1970s. Annual sea kayak symposiums have sprouted up across the country; the one last year at Port Townsend, for example, drew 700 people to seminars and demonstrations that ranged from "Tides and Currents" to "Zen of Kayaking." Tour operators now offer trips to North America's sea kayaking hot spots, which include the desert shorelines of Baja California, the wooded isles and passages of the Northwest, Maine's rocky coast—where paddlers have established a 350-mile "sea kayak trail"—the Caribbean and, increasingly, inland waterways such as the Great Lakes. (A good source of information on routes is *Sea Kayaker* magazine, published in Seattle.)

Compared with, say, whitewater kayaking, sea kayaking draws a somewhat older crowd—paddlers in their 30s, 40s and 50s, some of whom, one guesses, are former whitewater kayakers who no longer hanker for the Class IV rapids and adrenaline bursts of their younger days. It also attracts a higher proportion of women than some outdoor sports do. "The trips that I've led always have more women than men," says Mary Van Cline, a kayak guide and glass sculptor. A whitewater kayaker herself, Van Cline sees whitewater kayaking and downhill skiing as technically demanding, high-speed sports, while sea kayaking's reflective nature more closely resembles cross-country skiing. "You stop, float, look at what's happening around you."

It's easy to learn the simple paddle strokes of sea kayaking, and you don't really need any more than a normal sense of balance to get started and paddle with a tour group. For more ambitious kayaking, however, you'll need to learn things like self-rescue techniques and an Eskimo roll. You'll also need to study up on currents, tides, wave patterns, navigation, and a host of other nautical considerations. For some boaters, this is part of sea kayaking's attraction. "I tell people it's a cerebral activity," says Ken Fink, who got into the sport as an oceanographer at the University of Maine. "You have to ask, 'What's it going to be like when I paddle around the headland instead of in the bay? How big are the waves going to be today?' Your eyes are 26 to 28 inches above the water, and you're sitting down in it." Van Cline characterizes sea kayaking as "low-tech." "You actually have to get out there and work," she says. "It attracts a different type of person—someone who's not interested in getting someplace by speed."

We were getting no place by speed. I was learning that narwhal hunting is a game of endless waiting. Mamarut floated silently out among the spinning floes, and the narwhals' breathing filled the air. We still couldn't see them but knew they were working their way inland through the broken, melting ice floes, drawn to the rich food of the inner fjord. Tukummeq scanned the channels with binoculars and spotted black humps glinting in the sun, far off.

She pointed to three narwhals that were swimming up an ice passage toward our camp, their black shiny backs dolphining through the sea at a jogger's trot. Rhythmically bobbing closer, they looked enormous, bigger than our motorboats. That's when

Mamarut appeared. I couldn't see from where. It was as if he'd sprung out of the background of glacier-crested headlands, a floating chunk of ice that had jumped to life. He swung his kayak into the wake of the trailing narwhal.

We stood frozen, not whispering or moving, as Mamarut's arms pumped furiously, his paddle blades flicking from side to side. Slowly he gained, the kayak moving swiftly and soundlessly through the wake cast off by the narwhal's undulating tail. The animal remained oblivious. The gap shrank to about 75 feet. I sensed a hesitation in Mamarut's pumping stroke, and I watched for him to pluck the harpoon from his deck. In that instant, the eerie breathing burbled like water leaving a drain. The glassy surface closed over the shiny backs, and as the three narwhals simultaneously dove for safety, a frozen silence once more filled the luminous Arctic air.

On the Surface: Snow and Ice

A Short Stroll in the Firnspiegel

It begins when a high-flying speck of dust—windborne clay, forest fire ash, or even meteor dust from outer space—enters a well-chilled cloud and triggers the kind of disturbance you might expect if Madonna showed up at a teen dance party. The water molecules inside that cloud, until then jumping around in a "supercooled" frenzy of anticipa-

tion, suddenly lock arms in rings of six molecules and glom onto
the dust speck.

These hexagonal rings combine to build the honeycombed
structure of an ice crystal, an object that changes shape with the
versatility of an old Shakespearean actor working his way
through the Bard's canon. If the cloud temperature happens to
hover around -25°C, the crystal grows into a menacing, razor-
sharp prism; at -15°C it blossoms into a frilly star; and at -8°C it
folds duplicitously inward like a conspirator in a cape to create a
six-sided column that's absolutely hollow.

These prisms, stars, columns, plates, and needles—the basic
shapes of a snow crystal—tumble down through warmer, wetter
cloud layers where they stick together in jumbled clumps, balls,
and the perfect six- and twelve-sided stars we call snowflakes.
After an earthward journey of a few minutes to several days,
they'll pile chin to knees on the ground where they still refuse to
relinquish their change-artist nature. A snow particle might assume hundreds more shapes and textures until spring's warmth
finally administers its coup de grace.

If poet William Blake discovered an entire world in a single
grain of sand, in a snow crystal he surely could have found a thousand worlds. It's no wonder that snow, quite unlike sand, tends to
obsess those who come to know it. These include the great German astronomer Kepler, who wrote a mathematical treatise on the
six-cornered snowflake, and a Vermont dairy farmer named W.A.
"Snowflake" Bentley who spent forty winters in his barnyard with
a box camera, capturing over 5,000 stunning portraits of snow.

These two embraced snow as something that's a lot more than
the heavy white stuff at the far end of a shovel. But if to know
snow is to love it, to know it well you must first learn its names.

The following is a glossary that includes names conferred over the centuries by those who have worked, traveled, or played in it: Swiss farmers, Norwegian *langlaufers*, Eskimo hunters, Russian peasants on the snowblown steppe, as well as alpinists and skiers.

For each named snow type, however, probably hundreds of other crystal shapes and snowpack textures remain unrecognized. Fortunately, there are "snow poets" out there like Emil Tanner who attempt to rectify this deficiency. A Colorado architect and backcountry skier, Tanner and his ski buddies christen snow types they encounter in the high country with household names, such as that particularly soft, comfortable, pillowy type of powder, which they've dubbed "living room furniture."

"Any kind of hard crust and you go straight to the kitchen," says Tanner. "Formica . . . tile . . . linoleum. . . . It's fun to ski even the worst conditions if you can put a name on it."

DRY SNOW

COLD SMOKE (aka "champagne powder")—Slang for the very lightest, fluffiest snow that powder skiers seek with the fervor of knights after the Holy Grail—mistakenly, it turns out.

Cold smoke originates in cold, dry clouds where the temperature hovers around -15°C and permits the growth of "stellar crystals," as those star-shaped crystals are known to scientists. Joining together in flakes as they fall, they manage, unlike so many snowflakes, to escape a heavy shellacking with frost, thanks to the cloud's lack of humidity.

If they arrive on Earth on a cold, windless day, these spiky flakes and crystals stack up so tall and delicately on fence posts and ski slopes that their mass is about 98 percent air (known as 2-percent density snow). To walk through this fluff is to walk knee-deep through a layer of rustling, white air. Contrary to the skiers' myth, however, this fantastically light snow doesn't always make the best powder skiing because if it's *too* light, your skis, instead of floating, plunge down like a pair of iron bars to strike the hard-pack beneath.

Advises Alta Ski Patrol Director Gus Gilman, who quite possibly deals with more light powder annually than anyone on the planet: "The most awesome powder skiing you can have is a storm that starts off and fills in the moguls with about a foot of fairly dense snow, say 10-percent density, and then works up to a layer of 2-percent density snow. And you don't want it *too* deep. About thirty inches. That way it's hitting you about neck level instead of constantly flying up in your face and you can't breathe."

GRAUPEL—As opposed to the airiness of cold smoke, graupel means "granular" in German. Its pellets look like tiny styrofoam balls and are called "soft hail" by meteorologists. It forms when thick frost—or "rime" as it's known technically—cloaks a needle, column, or stellar crystal as it drops through a cloud. Along with rime, graupel particles pick up enough static electricity on their tumble earthward to buzz on impact with a radio antenna. Those few skiers lucky enough to have carved turns into a rare accumulation of "deep graupel" report that this bizarre substance is great, bouncy fun—like skiing down a mountain of packing material.

WINDBLOWN SNOW

SASTRUGI—Not some Japanese version of pasta, sastrugi is actually a Russian word for windblown snow. Though the word technically describes crescent-shaped drifts that are the polar equivalent of sand dunes, sastrugi sometimes refers simply to wind-patterned or wind-sculpted snow.

Snow that has been blown and packed by the wind serves as the reinforced concrete of the North. Think of all those delicate snow crystals—needles and stars and columns—that have fallen softly to the ground to form a fluffy snow cover. A gale wind rises, tumbling the snow particles over and over so that their little arms snap off. When they finally come to rest in a snowdrift, the limbless grains now can squeeze tightly together and bond into a firm mass like frozen baby peas packed in a cardboard carton.

The Inuit call this firm, windbeaten snow "upsik" and slice it into blocks that they stack up to make igloos. On sunny winter days, the sun-worshipping Swedes look for windpack to build U-shaped windbreaks as outdoor tanning salons. Some skiers refer to windpack as "pool-table snow" because it feels smooth and hard but slightly fuzzy under their steel edges, and allows them to track as true as a cue ball rolling over felt. Climbers hanker for a similar stiffly textured snow known as "styrofoam," in which they can kick in the front points of their crampons to climb steep, snowy faces as easily as they could mount a ladder.

SNIRT—A term used by the snowplow operators of Cavalier County, North Dakota, to describe the mixture of snow and dirt that appears on county roads when winter gales "get the fields moving." Windblown snirt, a substance NASA might find somehow useful, deposits in "pillow drifts" that are so hard, says county blade operator Ben Perius, that "you can drive a grain truck loaded with 400 bushels of wheat right over the top and never make a mark."

WET SNOW

CINNAMON ROLLS—There must be some cheap joke in here about whether snow scientists get enough to eat, but let's just say that this formation is known technically as a "snow roller." It occurs on "sticky" days when a bit of snow drops from, say, a branch, rolls down a steep slope, and accumulates spiraling layers until it flattens into an albino pastry.

A cinnamon roll is a sure sign that the snow conditions are perfect for building snowmen or hurling snowballs. Imagine a fluffy layer of new-fallen snow warmed with sun or balmy air until it just starts to melt. The meltwater fills the tiny hollow spaces called "capillaries" that lie between the snow particles, explains snow researcher Sam Colbeck. Now pick up two mittenfulls of that snow and press them together into a ball. Surface tension allows the meltwater in the capillaries of one mittenful to jump across in tiny bridges to join the meltwater in the other, so the snowball "sticks" together. This process is aided by the pressure you apply with your hands, which helps melt the snow particles together.

Any wet snow will "pack," but snow that's wet and *new* (read fluffier) contains more capillaries than snow that's wet and *old* (grainier); new wet snow is the tightest-packing high-caliber ammo for a snowball fight. This sticky snow will wreak havoc with a pair of cross-country skis, however, because it adheres to them like gumbo clay to a tractor tire. Norwegian racers prevent clingy buildup by "rubbing" a toothed scraper across their ski bottoms to gouge out tiny plastic hairs, explains Trond Benum, a Norwegian native and ex-University of Colorado racer. Norwegian competitors know this sticky, problematic snow—wet and fresh and about 0°C (32°F)—as "rubbe føre," which literally translates "rubbing condition," although Benum has heard American racers simply call it "hairy."

CRUSTS, ICE, AND "OLD" SNOW

SKARE ("scare-ah")—Another word from those fun-loving Norwegians; this one means a crust caused by a warm spell or rain, followed by a cold snap. For cross-country skiing it's so fast and firm, says Benum, that, given a stiff wind, a skier can hold open his parka like a spinnaker and sail across the Scandinavian countryside.

Crusts form as the snow cover ages or, as the physicists put it, "metamorphoses." Consider that fluffy, new-fallen snow again. Even if it simply lies there in the cold without any outside influence—without the warmth of sun or rain or the tumbling caused by wind—those stars, needles, columns, and what-have-you will change shape of their own fickle volition. Differences in vapor pressures cause water molecules to jump off the snow crystals' pointed arms and fill in their crevasses so the particles become rounded. The weight of the snow above presses particles more closely together and helps form ice bridges called "sinters," which link the particles. Under a magnifying glass, old snow looks like tiny clumps of glass beads joined by little glass necks.

Should winter never lift, the particles would compact over several years into the beginnings of glacial ice, or "firn." But, thankfully, warm spring sun triggers a cycle of daytime thaws and night-time freezes that melts and refreezes the smaller beads so they merge into the larger beads, which finally grow into kernels. By mid-March, skiers can slap on the suntan lotion, roll up their shirtsleeves, and cut long, arcing sprays across that delightful granular surface that's known as "corn."

FIRNSPIEGEL—Loosely translated from the German as "glacier mirror," it describes a thin skin of clear ice that covers the snowpack and causes deliciously hallucinatory phenomena.

The conditions that cause firnspiegel are as delicate and ephemeral as the substance itself. As the sun climbs in spring, its intensifying radiation penetrates the upper-most snowpack and melts its surface. At the same time, cool winds moving over it refreeze the water into a delicate skin of ice. This acts like the glass of a greenhouse, trapping warmer air and further melting the snow beneath.

The ice glaze reflects the low-angle light of sunrise or sunset like a mirror so that whole fields and mountainsides appear ablaze with "glacier fire." Beyond its beauty, you'll find few more satisfying remedies for pent-up frustration than a short stroll in firnspiegel; its shattering and tinkling give you the illusion of stomping across a long tabletop of fine china.

PENITENT SNOW—This is snow that forms tall, drooping snowcones that look like hooded monks kneeling at prayer.

Nieve penitente was named by Spanish-speaking explorers in the Chilean Andes, who, thrashing their way across vast fields of these tightly-spaced cones, must have felt like penitent sinners sentenced to flagellation. The phenomenon is unique to high altitudes in the tropics, where intense sunlight melts deep pits in the snowpack, leaving spiky towers up to ten feet high. The towers, in an attempt to present minimal surface area to the hot sun, typically point directly toward the sun's position at its noon-time zenith.

Our mountains produce miniature versions of these pits and towers known as "sun cups" or "ablation hollows." But the sun won't do the trick if the snow is especially dirty. Then warm winds gouge out the hollows; dirt particles naturally migrate to-ward the tiny ridges, insulating the high spots and allowing the wind to eat ever more deeply at the hollow's center.

BULLETPROOF OR BOILERPLATE—The old terms for New England's infamously icy ski conditions, which, according to Eastern skiers, are infrequent today because New England ski areas have pur-chased more snowmakers and grooming machines than Rommel had tanks. "Ice is something we don't have at Stowe," laughs pa-trol chief Bill Westermann. "Ice is something that goes in your cocktails."

Ice *particles* are another matter, however, because these form the basis of man-made snow. Water is "shattered" into tiny droplets as it is shot into the cold atmosphere through a power-ful fan or a compressed-air gun. Snow-makers strive for particles about 500 to 1,000 microns in diameter, or about the size of the head of pin, according to John Parker of Snowmax Technologies. Extremely fine particles of around 100 microns can make for supremely velvety skiing, but they don't fall easily to earth; one Midwestern resort accidentally iced up an airport runway—thir-teen miles from its snow guns.

Man-made snow typically costs around $1,000–2,000 per acre/foot, says Parker, but grows dearer with warmer and more humid weather, because snow makers must use more compressed air to freeze the water. This is where Snowmax, an additive to snow-making water, can save a snow maker money, according to adver-tisements. Absolutely pure water won't freeze until -40°C, but if dust specks or other impurities are present (remember, the Madon-na factor), they'll attract those supercooled water molecules at, say, - 15°C or higher, and cause them to freeze into ice crystals.

Certain nuclei work at higher temperatures than others, and Snowmax, according to the company's Senior Engineer Pat Ward, contains an ice nuclei so efficient it is able to freeze water as high as -3°C. (With ice as its nuclei, water freezes at 0°C.) Snowmax consists of a harmless (and dead) bacterium, *pseudomas syringae*, which contains a protein that draws water molecules to it in a pattern closely resembling the crystal lattice of ice. Ironically, this very common ice-making bacterium was discovered not on some snowy mountain slope, but in the Midwestern flatlands on the frost-damaged spots of corn.

CLEAR ICE, BLACK ICE, WHITE ICE—These are kinds of ice that occur, respectively, on a pond, on a highway, and in the ice-maker of your refrigerator.

The latter—white or cloudy ice—poses a particularly vexing problem to manufacturers of major appliances. To create perfectly clear ice cubes, explains Jerry Sturgeon, manager of refrigerant systems design at General Electric, in Louisville, Kentucky, you must build the cube in thin layers. If it freezes in a single block, the center solidifies last, expands, and shatters the surrounding ice jacket with tiny cracks, turning it cloudy. Making a layered cube requires several thousand dollars in additional equipment; this is why your local restaurant provides clear ice for your drink and your own refrigerator kicks out cloudy ice.

HOAR FROST AND RIME

SUGAR SNOW—Sweet it's not. Also known as "depth hoar," sugar snow sends chills through climbers and backcountry skiers because of its propensity to avalanche. With virtually no bonds holding its grains together, a handful of this stuff pours loosely through your gloved hand like sugar crystals.

By definition, all "hoar" snows form through sublimation: water passes from the vapor to the solid state without becoming a liquid. Jack Frost paints the windowpane with water vapor that freezes directly out of the air on cold nights, like dew. Depth hoar, as its name implies, occurs deep within the snowpack when water molecules migrate from warmer to colder layers and reform into ribbed crystals that, under a magnifying glass, look exactly like the Great Pyramid. In their attempt to transfer heat from the warmer to colder layers, the water molecules land on the hoar crystal itself rather than jumping into the crevasses between crystals, so they don't form "sinters," the little bridges of ice that normally bond snow particles together.

Despite the anxiety its unconsolidated nature causes mountain travelers, sugar snow has served the inhabitants of the flatlands well. One of its odd properties is that when it's "sifted" and left to sit in the cold, its grains *will* bond together into hardpack. The Native Americans of Canada's North Woods exploited this property by shoveling sugar snow into a mound with a snowshoe; they let it set up for an hour or two, then hollowed it out to create a conical, overnight shelter called a *quin-zhee*.

CAULIFLOWER—This is frost that grows on cliffs in giant lumps that resemble the vegetable. Extreme skiers bestowed this name after encountering acres and acres of the stuff in the Alaskan Coastal Ranges. It's found in maritime climates where supercooled droplets inside a cloud collide with a surface like a rock or a tree and freeze into thick layers of rime (the scientific term). A "snow ghost" is a Northwestern term for a stunted, mountaintop evergreen tree coated with several feet of this rime. Extreme skiers love cauliflower's soft but firm consistency because it allows their edges to bite easily—not unlike a sharp knife through steamed vegetables—and hold to 60°-plus slopes where they'd otherwise slip. "Skiing cauliflower is like 5.10 rock climbing," says skier Doug Coombs, "except you're heading down instead of up."

CHANDELIERS—Rare, dreamy stuff. "Surface hoar" (its real name) consists of large feathers of frost up to two inches high deposited by water vapor on the snow surface during cold, clear nights. These large feathers also form in glacial crevasses, along steamy streams, and in freezers if they are left undisturbed for weeks on end.

One enthusiast describes skiing surface hoar as a "triple rush" because of: 1) the rustling sound it makes as you skim through it; 2) the way it flicks up against your ski pants and tickles your calves; and 3) because it refracts the morning sun into rainbow sparkles like the glass prisms of a chandelier.

The Care and Use
of Perfect Ice

When I look back on my childhood winters, I realize how profoundly my approach to ice has changed. Skating was only a part of our activities back then, subordinated to the game of ice itself. Sure, we'd come home from school, lace up, and cut a few turns around the bay, but soon this wholesome pleasure would dim, and we'd move on to experimentation with the tensile strength of two inches of black ice when subjected to the impact of say, a 25-pound boulder. What satisfaction to hoist that rock overhead and spike it through the ice, shattering it into spiderwebs of cracks and a geyser of spray. A tinkling of ice fragments and splatter of water would spill around the black, upwelling rent, and beneath the ice, air bubbles would pulse like giant amoebas.

As we grew older we channeled this innocent energy into more formal games of our own devising—Icebreaker, the Ax-Chop Game—until finally giving it over to the controlled chaos of pickup hockey. No boundaries contained the play. The action sometimes roamed a quarter-mile from the goals, a tornado of flailing bodies, flashing sticks, and skittering dogs, as the drumbeat of skate blades echoed among the naked trees and frozen hills.

I still play pickup hockey, every winter afternoon at four. The players are older, and if we're not necessarily wiser or quicker than we were as kids, at least we sometimes pass the puck. Our game—Old-Guy's Hockey, I call it—still offers that exhilarating rush down-ice with the puck on your stick, the cold air wheezing in your lungs, the sweat pouring off you, your missed shot on the goal. We play a genteel adult version that proscribes body-checking and lifting the puck, the same rules as when we were kids, though now violations bring bruises and aches never known in childhood. And now, as Old Guys, our games themselves have taken on a patrician air, and we welcome newcomers, beginners, women, youths.

Other things have changed, as well. These days I live in the mountains, where water hurries downhill without pooling into lakes, and large, snowless sheets of ice are rare. Instead of roaming freely, ice play is now bounded by a rink, which we must manufacture ourselves. Where I once used my winters to invent new ways to smash ice, I now find myself cultivating the stuff, spending part of the cold months wearing a pair of pac-boots and getting shoved around the rink by the back-pressure of a fire hose.

There is only one good kind of ice—smooth and hard—yet there are dozens of varieties of the bad stuff. Any pond skater remembers those whitish-gray domes that appear suddenly on the frozen surface overnight, as hard and polished and mysterious as a substance from another planet. Your skates go clickety-clack as you bump over them, and when the puck hits them it goes winging off into a snowdrift. Even good, hard lake ice can crack when it contracts in very cold weather, causing fissures that tend to get chiseled into little chasms by the action of hockey-skate blades. When the opposing team attacks and you must skate backward to defend your goal, the chasms grab your skates and smack you down onto your tailbone or—best to wear a helmet—your head.

Flooding a homemade rink with a fire hose can produce a particularly unpleasant type of ice if the water drains away in patches, leaving only a skin of ice over a layer of air. You'll see a hockey game buzzing along at high speed until the puck suddenly hops about and the skaters stumble and flail and skate blades clash with a sound like meat cleavers going through racks of wineglasses.

Maybe it's by necessity that I've discovered a kind of serene pleasure in the making of good ice. As suburbanites find religion in manicuring a quarter-acre of Kentucky bluegrass, I've come to realize that the quest for the perfect sheet of ice is its own reward. We start with the first snowfall of early December, when our group of schoolteachers, stonemasons, wheat farmers, and college professors shows up in the grassy, kidney-shaped depression at the local park. We pack the snow with a lawn tractor to provide an undersurface, then set out a lawn sprinkler and run it for two days until the rink accumulates an inch or so of base ice. To this we apply the skating ice in thin layers (the key to adherence) with a spray-nozzle fire hose. This requires a marathon, round-the-clock session in which teams of ice-makers return home encrusted like wooly mammoths just spit out of the bottom of a glacier. After the rink is in play, we resurface it regularly with a fire hose or with the homemade Zamboni we rigged up by placing a propane stove in a lawncart and bolting on a cattle trough. As this contraption is towed along, a swatch of flowered curtain fabric drags behind it to smooth the flow of warm water over the old, pitted surface.

I take deep satisfaction in returning in broad daylight after a nighttime flooding session to find the ice—rare day!—smooth as a sheet of glass, free of bumps and chunks, unmarred by paw prints, bike treads, or cottonwood leaves. The surface, almost frighteningly fast under your gliding blades, screeches like fingernails on a chalkboard when you jam to a stop in a shower of ice shavings. Even during warm spells or blizzards, I find myself heading up to the rink at 4 P.M. whether or not there is a game. I shovel snow, or pack the drifts along the sidelines into "boards," or patch holes in the ice. I tell myself that I'm receiving a good upper-body workout, but really I want to nurture that sheet of ice, cultivate it, make it grow.

The Search for the Perfect Sled

The problem was that we broke too many sleds. It's not surprising, really. We are, after all, decades older—though perhaps not wiser—than your average sledder, and our aging frames carry plenty more flesh. Our sled run was no lightweight, either: a treacherous, twisting, quarter-mile chute that was capable of thrashing both sled and driver.

The sled run was my friend Steve Krauzer's bright idea. One gray winter afternoon, Krauzer—normally a hardworking novelist and responsible adult—pulled the plug on his word processor, seized a shovel, and marched out through snowdrifts to his Missoula, Montana, backyard. Packing the snow into curving ridges, he built a small sled run.

Later, with the help of friends, Krauzer lengthened the course, expanding it up the lower flanks of Mount Jumbo, a grassy, rounded mountain that rises behind his house. It was a run that offered a leg-punishing exercise on the way up, and on the way down a wild-eyed, snow-spraying ride that terminated with a tumble into a snowbank near the window of Krauzer's vacant office. It was the perfect antidote to the mid-winter blues.

Surprisingly, our bodies usually withstood the pounding; our sleds, however, did not. It was this that finally sent us on our quest: the search for the sled that could handle rough treatment, tight turns, and Jumbo's fickle snows. The search would send us scouring through secondhand stores, poring over toy catalogs, browsing through libraries, and consulting with sledders from several countries. We would learn that, over thousands of years, the sled has evolved from one man's first vehicles into one of his most sophisticated toys. And we would learn that its scope is enormous, embracing everything from bone-runnered sledges to $12,000 Italian-built racing bobs, virtual cruise missiles mounted on steel runners.

From the start a bobsled was out of the question (too costly and it needs an iced track), but we planned to test any other sleds we could lay our hands on. And when we found the perfect sled, we planned to haul it to the very peak of Mount Jumbo, and from there we would plunge 1,368 vertical feet to Krauzer's backyard.

In some respects, history has shunned the sled as if it were some rustic country cousin and instead has bestowed its laurels on that much younger sophisticate, the wheel. Centuries before the wheel's arrival, however, the sled hauled freshly killed game through the forests of northern Europe, where prehistoric wooden runners have been unearthed from bogs. Nor was it confined to lands of snow and ice; 4,000-year-old stone carvings portray Sumerians, Assyrians, and Egyptians hauling giant stone blocks and statues on sledges.

On dry land, of course, a sled creates a lot of friction; some carvings depict workers pouring lubricant beneath the runners—water, or possibly milk, its butterfat acting like oil. Others show the sledge runners rolling over rounds of wood. Appearing about 3500 B.C., the wheel surpassed the dry-land sledge, except on particular terrain (witness the horse-drawn farm sledges called stone boats).

In one situation, specifically, the sled was tough to beat—on snow and ice. Ice ranks as one of the slipperiest substances known. Its slickness may result partly from a lubricating layer of water that forms under the pressure or frictional heat of sled runners, as well as from partial rotation of molecular bonds in which water molecules act almost like roller bearings. So, on ice, the sled became the most efficient way to haul heavy cargoes.

Throughout the globe's northern regions, the sled, over millennia, developed in its many permutations: the dogsled of the Eskimos, the toboggan of the North American Indians, the Laplanders' *pulka*—shaped like a sawed-off canoe and towed by reindeer.

In the snowy parts of Europe, sleds eventually were hauling

everything from manure to royalty, the latter riding in horse-drawn sleighs carved in shapes of dragons, swans, and other beasts. The sleigh's popularity spread: Russians bundled up in three-horse troikas, while Americans dashed about in cutters. There were booby hutches, shifters, and driving sleighs, not to mention pungs, pods, and pony sleighs.

But Krauzer and I weren't much interested in pungs or pods for our high-speed slide down Jumbo. In this, we simply were following the age-old impulse that prompted Indian boys to fly downhill on sleds of wood or bone, and those Roman soldiers who, with spears for steering poles, supposedly rode their shields down the snowy passes of the Alps.

Despite the antiquity of the concept, however, it wasn't until the late 19th century that downhill sledding flourished as an organized sport and sled design blossomed into high art. Since then, sleds have appeared in dozens of styles, shapes, colors, sizes, but our research revealed that most fall into one of three major groups. In turn-of-the-century Europe, these groups were designated by nationality: a sled then was known as either an American, a Canadian, or a Swiss. Krauzer and I decided we'd better try one of each.

The American sled we knew intimately from our New England and Midwestern boyhoods. It's that long, low model, sometimes called a clipper, that's ridden belly-whopper style. This means headfirst, straight downhill, as fast as possible.

The American version of "coasting" extends back into the Colonial era; Boston Common already was a favorite sledding hill by the time of the American Revolution when British soldiers, camped on the Common during the winter of 1775-76, destroyed the sled runs. This wanton act prompted the boys of

Boston to take their grievances to General Gage, the British commander.

"What!" he replied. "Have your fathers been teaching you rebellion, and sent you here to exhibit it?"

The boys responded that they hadn't harmed the general's troops yet the soldiers persisted in destroying the sled runs and "we will bear it no longer!" The general, admiring their "love of liberty," promised that the sled runs would be left alone.

"All coasting in those days was racing, pure and simple," wrote James D'Wolf Lovett of his Boston boyhood in the 1850s. "Prominent sleds were as well known among the boys as racehorses and yachts are today." He describes sleds built of polished black walnut and upholstered in enameled leather bordered by gold tacks, materials suitable for a fine piece of furniture. Their names—*Raven, Comet, Flying Cloud*—reflected the owner's hopes for a fast descent, and their runners—the key to speed—were forged of the best "silver steel" and "kept burnished like glass." As one writer put it, "A slow sled was worse than none."

The earlier American sleds tended toward stubbiness and stout, solid-wood construction, or were improvised of items such as beef bones mounted on a board, or a single barrel stave to which a seat had been nailed. (This often uncontrollable contraption, known as a jumper or skipper, could send its rider spinning round "ker-whack into an apple tree" and was said to have no equal among the entire roster of sliding devices "for daredevil, exhilarating sport.")

With sledding's new sophistication in the latter part of the 19th century came not only an abundance of models, but also strict rules of behavior: racing headlong, boys went "bellywhacker" on clippers but girls "sat up straight," according to one obviously male memoir. "The ethics of society seeming to deny them the privilege of 'belly-buster,' and on high sleds—nothing could be more ignominious than a 'girl's sled,'—scraping and screaming, showing glimpses of red flannel petticoats as they prodded with their heels, acting much like frightened hens scuttling through a yard, they plowed to their goal."

Eighty-two-year-old Henry W. Morton remembers when "sleds had gender"; his family's company was building them. One of the nation's first sled makers, the Paris Manufacturing Corporation of South Paris, Maine, today is its largest. Presided over by Henry W's son Henry R., it was founded in 1861 by his grandfather, Henry F., who had hoped to go to college but suffered eyestrain from studying and took up sled building in his kitchen. The finished products were painted by his wife. The operation grew, and today collectors seek these kind of hand-painted sleds. "I've heard prices all the way up to $700 for a Paris sled that was maybe $3 when new," says Morton.

America's most famous sled is an old wooden clipper—*Rosebud*, a central symbol in the 1941 film *Citizen Kane*. The sled turned some heads a few years ago when film producer Steven Spielberg paid $60,500 at Sotheby's for a balsa-wood *Rosebud*. This, it turned out, was one of three copies made of the original hardwood *Rosebud*, which had been purchased for $12 shortly before *Kane's* filming. Two copies were incinerated during the making of the movie; the third, Spielberg's, eventually turned up in a studio warehouse. The original *Rosebud* apparently belongs to Art Bauer of Long Island, who in 1942 at the age of 12 was awarded it for winning an RKO-sponsored contest.

Early sleds like *Rosebud* had no steering devices; in the late 1880s that changed, thanks to Samuel Allen, a Philadelphia farm-implement manufacturer who is to the sled what the Wright Brothers are to the airplane. Allen invented the flexible-steering sled, since immortalized as the Flexible Flyer, a name stamped on the subconscious of almost any American who grew up near snow. Where riders previously steered by dragging toes or heels or by jerking the sled sideways, with Sam Allen's new sled you merely pulled the steering arm, thus bending the slender steel runners in the desired direction of travel. Eventually, the Flexible Flyer and sleds like it dominated the American sledding scene.

They still do. While in total volume American sled makers may now sell a greater number of plastic sliding devices such as saucers and trays, the flexible-steering clipper retains its title, king of America's sledding hills. You can look at this two ways: the American sled, little changed in 100 years, is stuck in the Dark Ages, or conversely, there's no need to improve upon perfection. Either way, Krauzer and I needed one; we found it at a local toy store, a five-foot-long Speedaway.

We were looking for a toboggan, too. The 1880s, a great decade for sledding on both sides of the Atlantic, also witnessed a tobogganing craze in the United States and Canada. Known in some circles as a Canadian, this Indian device had long hauled goods over North America's deep snows and had been adopted for military transport during the French and Indian War. British soldiers stationed in Canada (and obviously suffering from cabin fever) rode the capricious machines down hills. The sport became fashionable; tobogganists formed clubs, built giant slides, and wore costumes of bright wool blankets with waist sashes. By the 1890s, the tobogganing craze had subsided and coasting had reverted to its truest fans—the small boys and girls (who eventually overcame the stigma against bell-whacking) out for a chaotic afternoon at the local sledding hill.

All fall, Krauzer and I laid our plans. On sunny Indian-summer days, we hiked Jumbo's grassy flanks, scouting routes. Gloomy Saturday afternoons found us analyzing the sled inventories of local toy stores. Christmas approached and the deliverymen deposited several large packages at my door. I ripped them open to find some of the fanciest sleds I'd ever seen.

Everything was falling into place. Everything, that is, except snow. Looming above town, Jumbo stood nearly naked. Anxiously, we watched the skies.

Two adults eagerly awaiting sledding season, we seemed an oddity in America. But in Europe, sledding is serious sport that has been evolving steadily for the past hundred years; comparing the two is like comparing the kerosene lantern and the halogen lamp.

European sledding heated up in the past century when the fog-bound British discovered that the sun shone brilliantly in the Alps during the winter. Frequenting Switzerland's mountain spas, the British, always game, took to riding about on the little *hand-schlitten* (later known as a Swiss), the handsled that Swiss postmen took up and down the snow-covered mountain roads. It was exemplary sport, both for British gentlemen and their long-skirted ladies. Ernest Hemingway described the ex-military governor of Khartoum roaring along on a tiny sled, muffler blowing straight out behind him and a cherubic smile on his face: "It is easy to understand how the British have such a great Empire after you have seen them luge."

Then they started racing. Organized by British literary critic John Addington Symonds, the first international sled race took place down a two-mile road at Davos on February 12, 1883. Contestants rode European-style—sitting upright, their feet in front.

Only a few years later, however, in the 1887 running of the Davos race, a New Yorker by the name of L. P. Child easily outran the Europeans. Child, as one British sledding historian put it, possessed "that healthy disregard for old-established usage which is one condition of the progress of his nation." He won belly-whacking headfirst on an American-style clipper named *America*. No sooner had Child dismounted, writes T.A. Cook, "than every intelligent man realized the great advance that had been made."

A foolish tendency exists among sledders, as Krauzer and I soon discovered, to climb even higher up the hill. In nineteenth-century Switzerland, this manifested itself in the evolution of racecourses from simple mountain roads to treacherous ice-coated chutes. One of the first was the legendary Cresta Run at St. Moritz, site of a sporting ritual and social gathering that's still going strong a century later. During the 1880s, a fierce rivalry burned between the sledders of Davos and those of St. Moritz. So, with design help from a Swiss geometrician and under the supervision of Major W.H. Bulpett, the Cresta was build into a three-quarter-mile test of British mettle. It featured drop-offs called leaps, huge banked turns named Battledore and Shuttlecock, and straightaways where today's riders, belly-whacking on what are called Cresta sleds (Bulpett's design, a steel skeleton with movable seat), reach speeds of 80 miles per hour with their noses pushed down to within a few inches of the ice. Overlooking this bizarre scene is a glassed-in clubhouse where, as one rider puts it, "Europe's most elegant women, in their voluminous furs, sit sipping things."

But Mount Jumbo boasts no glassy clubhouses, and furs there

are worn by the occasional elk or bear. Krauzer and I rejected the Cresta sled as way too specialized for Jumbo's rugged slopes. We had other vehicles to consider, and much more to learn.

There was still another form of sled racing derived from riding the little handschlitten feet-first down mountain roads. Over decades, the roads became icy chutes, and the riders reclined to an aerodynamic, flat-on-the-back position. The sleds, gaining flexible runners manipulated with the feet, grew lower and wider, and sleekened into what are today's fearsome 48-pound racing luges. Inscribing perfect arcs across the walls of icy curves, withstanding the crush of a rider experiencing several g's, the luge is the Ferrari of the sledding world.

About 300 miles due north of Krauzer's backyard, near Calgary, a $15 million tube of concrete, lined with ice, coils down a slope like the tail of some giant white lizard whose ferocious bulk lies just over the hill. We stand next to the track and watch a luge shoot out of a turn, whistle past about six feet away at about 70 mph, and vanish into a tunnel-like curve.

At Calgary for a practice session is Wolfgang Schadler, a soft-spoken former Olympian from Lichtenstein, and the young, new coach of the U.S. National Luge Team. We have lagged behind the Europeans in competition as well as in the technique—essential for obtaining maximum speed—of preparing a luge's runners, or "steels." But the gap is narrowing in this art in which Schadler is an acknowledged expert.

"The roundest steels are the fastest," he explained over lunch one afternoon. Unlike sharp steels, he said, "they don't cut the ice and everything goes very smooth. But you cannot control steels that are too round. The sled goes *pssccccchhhh*"—he makes a wa-

vering motion with his hand. "You must find the middle, the op-
timum point that is sharp enough to drive a line and round
enough to go fast." Shaped with files and polished with diamond
paste, the edge must also take account of the luger's riding style
and body weight, as well as track configuration, ice temperature,
and other factors.

Another consideration in a luge's speed is air resistance. Try
holding your hand out a car window at 70 mph and you'll understand the reason for the sliders' shiny, skintight plastic suits, their
pointed boots—and why they climb into wind tunnels with their
sleds, seeking sleeker riding positions.

But frontal drag is only part of the aerodynamic problem, explained Karl Young, an engineer who has worked closely with
the U.S. team. Air washes over sled and slider and swirls about
behind, like the eddy made by a river washing over a rock. Called
turbulence drag, this hindering force could be reduced by adding
a tapered airfoil to the rear end of the sled, said Young. "If you
wore a conehead helmet—like on *Saturday Night Live*—you would
be very fast."

That's exactly what the West Germans, looking very egg-
headed, wore during the 1976 Olympics, but officials then
banned the helmets, citing safety reasons. With mere hundredths
of a second separating the winner and the also-ran, it is easy to understand why a luger will try anything. Many innovations have
been outlawed over the years by both luge and bobsled authori-
ties. "They don't want NASA coming in and designing a one-run-
nered sled with a computer balance system," explained Robert
"Bullet Bob" Hughes, marketing director of the Lake Placid-based
U.S. Luge Association. "They want it to look like a luge."

Sledding is taken seriously at Lake Placid, home to both a luge and a bobsled track. Most everywhere else in this country, though, sledding is the province of children. Compare this with Europe, where sledding ranks as a family sport and mountain resorts offer sled tracks as well as ski trails.

One popular European form of sledding, called *naturbahn*, represents a compromise between a light-hearted outing at the local hill and a high-g-force ride across the iced walls of a luge track. The name means natural track; without high-banked turns, the course consists of a snow-covered road, hiking trail, or curving track marked out on an open hillside, to be taken at speeds of 30 to 50 mph, often in a race against the clock.

There's no telling whether organized sledding will catch on here, though efforts are under way. We continue to associate sledding only with days when deep snows have sealed school doors shut; wild rides help us to escape life's cares as well as gravity.

The big day finally dawned. A storm had plastered Jumbo with fresh snow, but a warming trend crept close behind. It was now or never. On a Tuesday afternoon, towing two sleds each and carrying crash helmets, we slogged skyward through lingering shreds of storm cloud that wreathed the mountainside.

We knew where to go. A great hump rising above the city of Missoula, Jumbo was named after Barnum's elephant. A sled ride down its precipitous rear end or flanks would send us plunging either into Hellgate or Rattlesnake canyons, the former containing the twin concrete ribbons of Interstate 90, the latter cradling a sleepy neighborhood where folks probably wouldn't appreciate a sledder free-falling from the sky and plunging like an arrow into the backyard. But on Jumbo's "trunk," a gentle, open ridge, we'd found a route starting at about the top and winding nearly a mile, almost to Krauzer's back door. It presented only two major obstacles: a barbed-wire fence near the bottom, and a headwall midway that, in the lingo of the Cresta Run, we dubbed Dead-man's Leap. It was for this we carried crash helmets.

Mounting the ridge, we broke through the gray cloud bank into blue skies and bright sunlight. We began to sweat under the heat of the sun and the weight of the sleds that we'd picked so care-fully. Earlier, with a dozen eager friends, we'd tested our entire ar-senal: several flexible-steering clippers (nice, but breakable); a toboggan (fast, rugged, tough to steer); an old Swiss (built to last—I'd ridden it as a child); a bulletproof plastic number (we called it the SST, as in supersonic transport); and a high-tech German Swingrodel, sporting a hinged seat that flexed articu-lated runners (I've yet to master it).

For our big descent, I'd carefully considered a naturbahn luge, a sturdy, smooth-riding Cadillac of a sled, but in the end both Krauzer and I opted for that old standby—the clipper. On a clip-per, you can drag your feet behind. A clipper felt familiar. A clip-per felt *secure*. Yes, there was irony here. After our months-long international search, the model I ultimately dragged up Jumbo was a durable old Hiawatha Meteor that I'd picked up for $19.95 two years earlier at Paul's 2nd Hand Store.

We paused to rest halfway up Jumbo's trunk. Above us loomed the headwall of Deadman's Leap. We were both thinking the same thought: "Boy, are we gonna be hauling by the time we get there."

Finally, we stood on a knoll at the top of our run. Far below, clouds shrouded the valley, obliterating the city. Mountain peaks jutted from the soup. It was a view you'd expect from an airplane window, not a sledding hill. But the first guy down the Cresta Run probably had second thoughts too.

We tied padding to our sleds. Krauzer recklessly volunteered to go first.

We strapped on our helmets. Krauzer allowed how maybe he'd retire from competitive sledding if he survived this run.

We knocked snow from the runners. Krauzer asked me to tell his girlfriend that it had been a good—albeit short—life.

We shook hands and Krauzer picked up his sled, belly-whopped onto it and was gone. I caught a last glimpse of his boot soles as he disappeared round a bend. I could still hear the sled rattling over bumps and ruts. Then there was silence.

"Hey!" A voice floated up from below. "I'm stuck!"

Sitting at Krauzer's kitchen table drinking beer late that day, we analyzed our descents. We'd had some good bouncing plunges down Deadman's Leap—toes dragging, snow spraying—but on the flatter sections our sleds bogged down in the soft, wet snow. We'd successfully completed maybe half our route. What we really needed, we decided, was a good freeze. Maybe a couple inches of new snow. Or the fancy prototype sled I'd just seen, or maybe if we packed down the course regularly, or. . . .

Far above Krauzer's kitchen table, Jumbo looms, waiting for the perfect sled, the perfect snow.

The Ice League

By late November, all it takes is one cold, still night. Early the next morning we gather on the cobbled shore. Before us, glistening in the low winter sun, stretches a one-by-three-mile sheet of virgin ice—polished, flawless, sheathing the entire lake.

Someone tosses a rock: BONK . . . Bonk . . . bonkkkkk, it skitters out, its impact echoing in the wooded hills. It *sounds* solid. Someone else steps carefully off the shore. He shuffles out, open rubber boots flapping, hockey stick gripped in hand. The ice cracks and groans with every step.

He taps it with the hockey stick. Nothing happens. He taps harder. The stick plunges through and lake water burbles up, spreading out into a puddle. Satisfied, the tester shuffles gingerly back toward the shore, the thin ice bending visibly beneath his weight, a spiderweb of cracks shooting out around him.

"It's OK," he pronounces, hopping onto dry land. "As long as you keep moving."

These were the opening rituals of ice season, one of the best times of the year for someone growing up along a lake in southern Wisconsin. Part of the "ice belt" that takes in parts of Minnesota, Illinois, Michigan, Pennsylvania, New York, and New Jersey and continues around the globe, it is far enough north to ensure plenty of cold but far enough south to escape the deep, ice-burying snows. While it may not have much in the way of vertical ice—the glaciers and frozen waterfalls beloved by climbers—in terms of horizontal ice, southern Wisconsin, with its many lakes, boasts some of the world's finest.

I'm not talking about plowed rinks or milky slabs of the artificial variety. A lake full of clear ice—the much-vaunted "black ice"—is in a class of its own. It's almost unnatural, the perfection of this huge, absolutely flat surface, as smooth and polished as a ballroom floor, extending on and on, skate stroke after skate stroke, seemingly into eternity.

And it's irresistible. A lake full of smooth, unmarked ice is a blank canvas of possibility, tempting the human mind. Wordsworth knew all about this. He etched his name on the "glassy plain" with the traceries of his skate blades. Yet Wordsworth possessed a poetic imagination; when it came to frozen lakes, ours were demonic little minds.

There were distinct phases to the ice season. Early-season skating was a matter of acquainting yourself with the ice. This demanded several changes of clothing; we didn't consider ourselves on familiar terms with the ice until we'd fallen through it.

That opening day, we'd lace up our skates—me, my siblings, the neighbors, our cousins, whoever was around—and, sticking close to shore, would simply go exploring. Gliding over the transparent surface, you could peer down to the green-hued lake bottom and—as if gazing out an airplane window—watch an unfolding still life of logs, rocks, weed beds, sunken rowboats, and dark, mysterious holes in the mud that, according to one leading theory, were the lairs of man-eating snapping turtles.

We'd turn and swoop and spin and jump and bang around a hockey puck; inevitably, we'd dare each other to try the patches of *really* thin ice, a sport that demanded cool nerves to keep your weight equally distributed over both feet on the wildly cracking and bending ice, as well as the presence of mind not to stray over deep water.

Games like this, of course, have a way of escalating; skating on thin ice for us reached its ultimate form in what we called "the ax game," best played early in the season, when the ice is about two inches thick, and best played early in life, when one is younger and dumber. We'd pick a spot close to shore, where the water wasn't more than about waist-deep, trace out a circle about 15 or

20 feet in diameter, and, with an ax, chop along the perimeter until we had a free-floating ice floe. The object was to skate across it.

This was no great feat at first—as long as you moved quickly. It became much more difficult as the game progressed, however, because after each crossing someone would administer an ax chop to the ice floe. The first chop would split the floe in half, the next two would break it into quarters, the next into eighths, and finally into pieces so small that passing over them resembled tap dancing at high speed across a pond full of ice cubes. The game was over when someone—a younger sibling, for instance—took the big swim, scrambling out and making a dripping dash for the house.

(I sometimes wonder why we didn't die young. Activities like this, I should caution, would be very foolish over deep water and extremely dangerous on a frozen river, where the current can pull you under the ice.)

The next phase of the ice season—usually around the holidays—brought the large hockey games. Whole families would turn out on crisp, sunny mornings, the slower or older skaters taking the goals, girls and mothers on figure skates, boys and fathers on hockey skates, and the puck would sometimes get lost in a churning mob of skaters and sticks until someone could break loose toward a goal. At noon, nearly exhausted, we'd bask in sweat and the subtle warmth of the sun, chewing our half-frozen sandwiches, a knot of warm-blooded life on a sheet of cold crystal, the ice chips cut by our sharp steel blades sparkling like diamond flakes.

December's thickening ice also permitted iceboating and skate sailing, sports unknown to most of the world because they demand very specific conditions—wind sweeping across a large expanse of snow-free ice—that are very difficult to find in nature and impossible to reproduce. These sports also involve incredible speeds; on the polished surface of a frozen lake you're freed from the bonds of friction just as astronauts are released from gravity.

But we weren't much interested in the physics of ice; we were into its freedom, the headiest freedom of all being that of midnight iceboating, when you're released from friction as well as sprung from time and space, aware only of raw speed—a slender projectile wrapped in the scream of the wind and the roar of the runners, the pitches suddenly rising as the boat hikes up on two points. You keep it there, poised in the howling night at 60 mph, finally dropping it down and swinging into a screeching turn when you see the dark, looming band of the shore, returning to earth from somewhere far away.

Sometimes we had moonlight. One night, four of us, taking turns with the iceboat in the middle of the sparkling, snow-dusted lake, wordlessly and spontaneously started to wrestle, tumbling over and over in the powdery snow until, exhausted and panting, we lay on our backs looking up at the moonlit sky and heard the rumble of the returning boat. Then, switching pilots, we began the ritual again, as if in paganistic tribute to so beautiful a night and the simple joys of a frozen lake.

The early part of the ice season ended when the big snows blew in and we were forced onto plowed rinks, giving the rest of the lake over to a few ice fisherman huddling in their shanties. Yet the lake was still a source of much amusement; in the midwinter cold the ice did some very strange things.

One of the many unusual properties of water is that it expands considerably when it freezes, increasing in volume by 8 percent. As water freezes, its molecules arrange themselves into a lattice-work, forming a six-sided crystal (in lake ice the crystals generally grow into long columns, about as thick as your thumb). The molecules in this latticework have more space between them than the molecules in water's liquid state; thus ice takes up more volume. For this reason, of course, it floats on top of a lake.

What we liked about all this were the "ice heaves" caused by the process of expansion. These were long, narrow ridges, perhaps three feet high, where the ice's expansion had caused the lake's surface to buckle. On skates or even a bicycle, you could bank a turn off the ice heaves, or fly off them ski jump-style. You could smash them open with a big rock and look inside the glassy tunnel, or use them in a hard-hitting game of King of the Mountain. One of the abiding wonders of my youth also involved an ice heave—the time a friend relieved himself on a crack in the ice, which, as if in protest to this indignity, suddenly buckled up into a half-mile-long heave.

Terribly powerful, as anyone whose engine block has frozen and cracked will attest, the expanding ice also pushes against the shore, piling up low mounds of earth and stones. Sometimes you could watch a two-foot-thick slab grinding away at the concrete foundations of someone's boathouse, a small-scale version of a glacier chewing apart a mountainside.

Because ice reaches its maximum expansion at 32°F, as the temperature drops, it starts to contract slightly. On very cold nights it's this contraction that causes the ice to "boom," producing a haunting thunder that echoes across the lake. On a calm mid-winter night at 20° below, you stand quietly on the snow-dusted lake, while the booms and groans roll down the ice, the surface shifting slightly as they pass. Gripped by the ice and frigid air, a speck of warmth swathed in down, you listen to what it says.

Growing up on a Wisconsin lake, I developed a certain fondness for the substance itself, a substance that seems both sensual and abstract. You could call ice the original "miracle plastic." Take a big block of crystal-clear ice: You can carve it into sculpture, saw it into cakes or cubes, melt it into ice water, shatter it into diamond fragments, or, with enough time and pressure, you can actually bend it. It comes in a variety of colors—clear, blue, green, white—and in infinite shapes, the shapes of glaciers and frozen waterfalls, icebergs and icicles, ice caves and smooth midwestern lakes.

These are things you can climb up, skate over, or slide down, activities conducted on a medium that lies somewhere between dry land and deep water, yet somehow beyond them both. Listen to the satisfying crunch of steel-pointed crampons on a glacier, the solid thunk of a well-placed ice ax, or the ripping of a hard-driving skate blade; these are the songs of sports that celebrate a *medium* as much as a movement, sports that joyfully exalt nature's originality.

The ice season would end as suddenly as it had begun. With early spring the snow would melt off the lake, leaving it once again good for iceboating, and then the sun would go to work, seeming to drill tiny vertical tunnels into the thick layer. Caused by melting between the columnlike ice crystals, these tunnels would expand as the weather warmed until the ice was "honeycombed" and you could kick a hole through it, the broken chunks each a delicate sculpture, a tiny crystal city of tunnels and turrets and towers.

On a warm, windy March day—the opposite of the cold, still November night that had frozen the lake—the entire sheet would start moving, pushed by the wind. We'd come home from school and find mounds of honeycombed ice piling up on the shore, ice plowing into the sod, pushing rock and sand before it, big chunks of the thick, honeycombed layer flipping up onto dry land and shattering with the crash of windowpanes falling to the pavement.

The wind pressure on that sheet was enormous; it seemed that nature's hand had decided to clear the lake, wiping it clean of winter until, by day's end, nothing remained but waves on the lake, melting piles of ice on the shore, and the promise of spring in the air.